Factory Girl

Barbara Greenwood

Kids Can Press

For Page and Michael

Text © 2007 Barbara Greenwood

Kids Can Press acknowledges the financial support of the Government of Ontario, through the Ontario Media Development Corporation's Ontario Book Initiative; the Ontario Arts Council; the Canada Council for the Arts; and the Government of Canada, through the BPIDP, for our publishing activity.

Published in Canada by	Published in the U.S. by
Kids Can Press Ltd.	Kids Can Press Ltd.
29 Birch Avenue	2250 Military Road
Toronto, ON M4V 1E2	Tonawanda, NY 14150

www.kidscanpress.com

Edited by Valerie Wyatt
Designed by Julia Naimska
Printed and bound in Singapore

The hardcover edition of this book is smyth sewn casebound.
The paperback edition of this book is limp sewn with a drawn-on cover.

CM 07 0 9 8 7 6 5 4 3 2 1
CM PA 07 0 9 8 7 6 5 4 3 2 1

Library and Archives Canada Cataloguing in Publication

Greenwood, Barbara
      Factory girl / written by Barbara Greenwood.

ISBN-13: 978-1-55337-648-4 (bound)
ISBN-10: 1-55337-648-X (bound)
ISBN-13: 978-1-55337-649-1 (pbk.)
ISBN-10: 1-55337-649-8 (pbk.)

1. Child labor—Juvenile fiction. 2. Child labor—History—20th century—Juvenile literature. 3. Factory system—History—20th century—Juvenile literature. I. Title.

PS8563.R4177F32 2007   jC813'.54   C2006-902337-9

Acknowledgments
Immigrants to North America often found themselves working long hours for low pay in unhealthy conditions. This was particularly true of the thousands of young girls and women who worked as sweated labor in garment factories. For insights into that life, I am indebted to transcripts of testimony given at the trial of the owners of the Triangle Shirt Factory and posted on the Cornell University Web site at www.ilr.cornell.edu/trianglefire/. Valuable information was also found in David Von Drehle's *Triangle: The Fire That Changed America* (Atlantic Monthly Press, 2003).

Information about the life of urban slum dwellers was found in *How the Other Half Lives* (American Century Series, Hill and Wang, 1957) by Jacob Riis, first published in 1890, and *The Conditions of the Working Class in Toronto, 1900–1921* (University of Ottawa Press, 1979) by Michael J. Piva. Among many other studies of working class life, most helpful was *Childhood and Family in Canadian History* (McClelland & Stewart, 1982) edited by Joy Parr.

The period 1900 to 1914 is well documented in archival photographs. My thanks go to Elizabeth Cuthbertson, Archivist at the City of Toronto Archives, for her invaluable assistance in guiding me through their extensive visual record, and to Patricia Buckley, photo researcher extraordinaire, for her detective skills in tracking down compelling photos from both American and Canadian sources.

Thanks also to the excellent production team at Kids Can Press, particularly Julia Naimska, whose elegant design seamlessly weaves together the fiction and information components.

This book has had a lengthy gestation period. I could not have persevered without the constant encouragement, wise advice and discerning blue pencil of my long-time editor, Valerie Wyatt. And, as always, I thank my husband, Robert E. Greenwood, for his willingness to research one more elusive fact as well as his unfailing love and emotional support.

Kids Can Press is a **Corus**™ Entertainment company

Contents

CHAPTER 1

Looking for Work

Maybe this time …

Emily Watson peered in through the shop window. The afternoon sun made a mirror of the glass, forcing her to shade her eyes to see inside. A long counter ran along one wall. On top were glass cases holding trays of candies — mounds of chocolate balls, butterscotch pennies, peppermint lozenges. Emily's mouth watered. Halfway along the counter stood a cash register, its gold paint glinting in the sunlight. The lady behind it was plump and motherly. And she was alone. Emily glanced again at the small sign in the window: Help Wanted.

She tugged down her too-short jacket and smoothed her skirt. Then, taking a deep breath, she pushed open the door. The jingle of the bell startled her.

"Can I help you?" The woman's smile was friendly. A good beginning. The last one had frowned from the moment Emily had set foot in her store.

"I'd like …" Emily had to stop to clear her throat. "I'm here to apply for the job."

The smile vanished.

Emily rushed into her prepared speech. "I'm very good at arithmetic, and I really like to help people. I know I'd make a good saleslady."

"Too young."

"I'm older than I look. Nearly fifteen."

The eyes narrowed appraisingly. "Twelve if you're a day."

Emily pulled herself up to her full height. "I've finished school already. I'm old enough to work."

The woman's face settled into a tight, hard frown. "Don't you argue with me, my girl. I'm not about to get myself closed down for hiring a child."

Tears stung Emily's eyes. She had tried so hard, but in every shop she'd heard the same answer.

Sorry, the man in the bakeshop had said.

No openings. The grocery clerk hadn't even turned from stacking oranges.

Out! the haughty saleslady in the hat store had ordered.

"Now, now … Don't take on so." The voice was softer. Maybe … But when Emily looked up, the saleslady was still frowning. "There is one place." She pursed her lips in disapproval. "I don't hold with it, mind, but I've heard they hire underage girls. It's not what I'd want for my own daughter, but …"

"Please. I have to find …" Emily choked on her words.

"Now don't upset yourself again. Try the Acme Garment Factory. Just keep going down the street. It's at the bottom of Mill Lane."

A factory. She had so wanted to work in a nice, clean shop. Well, hours of trudging up and down Main Street had shown her how foolish that hope had been. But — a factory.

The doorbell jingled. "Be off with you, now," the woman said in a brusque undertone. Then she turned a smiling face to her customer.

Emily felt so tired she could barely drag herself from the shop. A factory at the bottom of Mill Lane. I'll go tomorrow, she decided. It was already late afternoon and she was sticky with sweat. Home. She wanted so badly the comfort of home. Then she remembered. Home wasn't home anymore. Not since yesterday. Would she ever scrub that picture from her mind? Mam in the lead pushing their old wicker baby carriage. Under, over and around baby Annie and wee Bertie she'd packed towels and sheets and pillows. Into Ernie's little pushcart they'd piled their few pots, pans and dishes. Emily had had to borrow a wagon to hold the wicker laundry basket full of neatly folded clothes. Bringing up the rear was their neighbor, Mike Magee, pushing his handcart piled with their chairs, a table, her mother's trunk, three tattered, flimsy mattresses and the boards to make up their beds.

Evicted! Because they couldn't pay their rent. Emily flushed hot with humiliation. That must never happen again. I must find a job. Now.

Squaring her shoulders, she turned her back on the friendly storefronts with their customers bustling in and out and headed toward a grimmer section of Main Street. Here she saw only the blank brick walls of tall buildings, their windows too high up to show any signs of human life. The street noises had changed, too, from cheerful chatter to the hollow clop of horse's hooves on cobblestones and the rattle of delivery wagons. Piles of trash teetering on the curbs and animal waste flung into the gutters gave off a sickly sweet smell. A furtive scurrying told her that rats were feasting. With a shudder she pulled her skirt tight around her legs.

How had it come to this? All year Miss Henderson had been telling the girls in Senior Fourth how women at last had a chance to make their mark in the world. Go on to Continuation School, she'd said, and the world will open up in front of you. That promise and Mam's encouragement had kept Emily working hard at her studies — until three days ago. The thought of that horrible day still made her feel sick.

At quarter to nine, she had crept into the school, desperate to find Miss Henderson before the bell rang and the halls filled with students. The doorknob rattled under her shaking hand and the teacher turned from writing on the blackboard, eyebrows raised in annoyance. Then she saw Emily and her severe expression softened. She reached out a hand. "Come in, Emily. What is it?"

"I … I …" Emily had to swallow before she could choke out the story — how she'd have to leave school that very day, a whole month before final exams, and find a job because her father … She couldn't bring herself to say it. How they hadn't heard from her father for months and now they'd run out of money.

She felt Miss Henderson's hands clasp her shoulders. The firm touch calmed her, comforted her.

"I want you to listen carefully, Emily."

She looked up and was locked into the intent gaze that had kept her working so hard that year.

"No matter what happens," her teacher continued, "remember this: To work, to earn your own living, means you can look at the world with pride. It's not the job, it's the way you do the work that counts. Don't ever forget, there is dignity in labor." She paused, and Emily blinked with the effort of concentrating on her words. Then Miss Henderson smiled. "You've done splendidly this year, Emily. You will get your graduation certificate — I promise you."

Emily had walked out of the classroom glowing, as though she were destined for the most exalted of futures. But now?

Dignity? Where was the dignity in being thrown out of every shop she'd tried? And what about this time? What if not even a factory wanted her? Then she spotted it. Just ahead, a sign high on a brick wall: Mill Lane.

Emily turned into the lane and was immediately plunged into a chilly darkness. Her sun-dazzled eyes peered down the narrow passage. Under foot, cedar block paving had given way to rotting planks laid over the mud of the lane. How could this be the place? But there on the pitted brick wall was another faded sign. Her eyes, now accustomed to the gloom, made out the hand-lettered words: First Floor — Everlast Shoes; Second Floor — Excelsior Matches; Third Floor — Acme Garment Factory. A dark opening in the wall showed four cracked stone steps leading to a door.

This was it. Her last try today. Emily took a deep breath and started up the stairs. The door creaked open at her touch, and she stepped into a square alcove lit by a dim electric bulb hanging from the ceiling. To her left was a door that said Everlast Shoes. A steady chunk, chunk, chunk made the floor vibrate. In front of her was a dark staircase. She started up. There was no railing, and the stairwell was so narrow that her shoulders brushed both walls. At a turn in the stairs her nose wrinkled from the sudden stench of sulfur. Excelsior Matches.

She hurried up to the next landing. On the door directly

in front of her the words Acme Garment Factory were barely visible through the grime on the frosted glass window. From inside came the metallic chattering of sewing machines. How easy it would be to run back down those dark stairs. And then what? Tell Mam she hadn't even tried? No, she couldn't disappoint Mam. Not when they were so desperate.

She pushed the door open. Noise roared at her. She clapped her hands over her ears, then noticed a bowler-hatted man behind a table counting bolts of white fabric. Beyond him, pale gray light from grimy windows showed a room crowded with row after row of sewing machines, their operators hunched over the jumping needles.

The man looked up and shifted a half-chewed cigar to one corner of his mouth. "Yeah?"

"I … I heard you were hiring." Emily felt as though her words were swallowed by the din of the machines, but the man turned and yelled down the room.

"Dolly, come and look at this one."

A young woman appeared carrying a half-sewn blouse, a style Emily recognized as a shirtwaist. She spread it on the table, then held out a pair of scissors. "Let's see you snip off those threads."

Emily scrubbed sweaty palms down her skirt, took the scissors and snipped.

The woman peered at the results. "Seems nimble enough. Yes, she'll do." She turned to Emily. "Be here at 7:00 sharp tomorrow morning and bring your own scissors."

"Does that mean I have a job?"

"For what it's worth," the girl said, too low for the man to hear. Then louder, "You'll get four dollars a week, with money deducted if you're late or you cut anything you're not supposed to. Seven sharp, mind. And bring your lunch. We don't finish until 6:15." She gathered up the shirtwaist and headed back toward the rows of sewing machines.

Emily stared after her. In all that long room not one head had turned to see what was happening by the door.

It took Emily half an hour to walk home. She started off in a daze, her ears still ringing from the noise of the clattering machines. She should feel happy — she had a job. Instead she felt heavy with despair. This shouldn't have happened. If only her father …

"I'll send you money every month, Lily," he'd promised Mam just before he'd taken off to search for work out west. "You know I won't fail you." And at first the money had come every month. Enough for rent and food and a bit left over. But now, for the third month in a row — nothing.

And then, last week, that stomach-wrenching scene in the post office. Mam crying, clutching at the metal grille of the wicket. "Please look again. It must be there. It must! Did you check in that bag?" Hot with embarrassment, Emily had begged her mother to come away, even though she knew how desperately they needed the money the missing letter would surely hold.

Stop! she told herself. You'll be crying in a minute. She shook her head to clear away the gloom and found she'd walked right past her turnoff. No point heading for the old neighborhood. That life was over.

She turned back and started down toward the train tracks where the houses crowded together along dingy laneways. With each street she crossed, the buildings grew smaller and shabbier. Coal-blackened brick gave way to stucco and clapboard, windows broken or gray with ancient dirt, doors scabby with peeling paint. The sour smell of garbage, rotting in the heat, made her stomach heave.

Clusters of thin, ragged children played on broken steps or in the gutters. Ahead of her trudged an odd little figure, bent gnome-like under a pile of blankets or perhaps coats. Emily had nearly caught up with it when she recognized the breeches on the short legs sticking out below the load.

"Ernie? What on earth?"

Her brother's face grinned up at her from under the load. "Sewing for Mam. Mrs. Magee told her about this place. Gosh, it was horrible, Em. I had to go down twisty old stairs to a smelly cellar and a man plopped this pile of stuff on me and said have it back by the end of the week. But it's okay, 'cause on the way I met up with a swell bunch of guys. And tomorrow we're going coal-picking."

"Coal-picking?"

"Yeah. Free coal, just for the picking. One of the guys, Alfie, says he'll show me how."

He shifted his load slightly and trudged on, seeming not at all upset or ashamed or any of the other emotions Emily felt roiling inside her. Almost as though it were a big adventure, living in this dreadful neighborhood.

Holding her nose against the stench from the row of privies, she followed him down the lane to the shabby little house they shared with another family. The door opened right into the front room. Her mother was sitting at the table wiping dribbled porridge from little Bertie's chin. She turned a hopeful look on Emily.

"I've got a job, Mam." Her mother's eyes lit up. "In a factory," Emily continued in a breathless rush. "Snipping threads … with two cents off for every wrong cut."

"A factory?" Her mother closed her eyes and pressed her lips tightly together.

She's going to cry, Emily thought. Then the tensions and humiliations of the day overwhelmed her, and she burst into tears herself.

EMILY'S PREDICAMENT

"How has it come to this?" Emily cried when she ended up working in a factory.

Emily was not resentful because she had to work. She had always known that she would have to bring in money to help her family. She was upset because she felt she had to go out to work too soon.

By 1912, in most of North America and certainly in the big cities, laws stated that children must attend school until they were fourteen. Emily had grown up expecting to stay in school that long. She hoped that having an education would make it easier for her to get a good job. She might become an apprentice learning a trade, such as hat-making, or train to become a telephone operator. Better still, she might be lucky enough to get one of the new office jobs opening up for women. With that extra bit of schooling, the world would be an exciting place.

But her family's poverty had flung Emily into the work world when she was only twelve, two years under the legal age to work. That meant the only job she could get — working in a factory — was unskilled, low paying and with little hope of advancement. She was not the only child in this predicament.

A child worker in a textile factory

Working Children

Children have always worked. Children who lived on farms helped with the chores. A four-year-old could scatter feed for the chickens. A ten-year-old could weed the corn. A twelve-year-old could plough a field. Older children could babysit the younger ones so that the adults could work. Farm children were useful from an early age.

Some factories operated twenty-four hours a day. In this glass factory, boys as young as ten worked the day shift one week and the night shift the next.

When families moved into the cities, the type of work that children did changed. Now, instead of family members working together on land they owned, they were forced to work away from their home in the one place that offered many jobs — factories. And right from the beginning of the industrial age, children, often as young as five, worked in these places, too.

Emily's family belonged to a large group at the bottom level of society called the working poor. Most of the adults had jobs, but the jobs paid so little that parents had to struggle to pay the rent and feed and clothe their children. The only solution was to send the children out to work. With many small amounts of money coming in, the family might just manage to survive. So, from an early age, the children of the working poor knew they would be expected to contribute to the family finances. They understood what was known as the "family contract" — an unspoken agreement that children would pay back their parents for the care they received when they were very young.

A childhood of being fed and cared for lasted only until the age of five. From six to ten most children attended school. For many poor families school was a place to send children while the parents were working. Children between ten and twelve became unpaid babysitters at home after school. If the mother worked in a factory, at least one child, usually the oldest girl, was kept home from school to tend her younger siblings. She also prepared meals each day and did general tidying and cleaning. This was how she paid her parents for their early care of her.

Depending on family circumstances, her brothers might be allowed to stay in school for a few more years, but from ten on they would have after-school jobs, selling papers, shining shoes or acting as messenger or delivery boys for stores and businesses. If boys couldn't get paying jobs, they scavenged, hunting through the garbage in well-to-do neighborhoods or garbage dumps, even stealing things left out in back alleys. Families who were desperate didn't ask where an extra chair or a slightly dented pot had come from.

At fourteen, or earlier if the family needed the money, children would go out to work full time. Boys might get jobs as laborers, but girls almost always went into factories. All through their teenage years, boys and girls lived at home and each week they gave 80 percent of their wages to their parents. With several teenagers working, families were better off than they had ever been.

By eighteen, children had paid back their debt to the family; they had fulfilled the family contract. Now it was time to work for themselves. In a few years, after saving a little bit of money, they were ready to get married. But with the arrival of the first baby, the cycle started all over again.

Children helped with the housework. With two parents working, everyone in the family had chores.

WHEN THINGS GO WRONG

Emily would never forget the day she heard the bad news. Dashing in from school, she saw her father's work boots standing in the front hall. Her heart jumped. Dad was never home this early. Voices led her to the tiny kitchen at the back of the house. From the doorway she could see her father slumped at the table, his head in his hands.

"Mam! What's wrong?"

Her mother turned a stricken look on her daughter. "It's the factory," she said. "They've laid off all the workers. Just like that. Your father's out of work."

So it had happened to them. Just like the Rileys and the O'Malleys in the next street. What would happen to them now?

Families like Emily's always knew they were living on the edge, with disaster lurking just around the corner. If a factory received few orders, workers were laid off. Or an accident could leave a worker crippled and unable to work.

Why did this spell disaster for a family like the Watsons? In 1912 workers were expected to look after themselves when things went wrong. Some might have tiny insurance polices they paid pennies into each week to help them over bad times. Most had nothing, and employers felt no obligation to help a worker who had been hurt. "I'm not a charity," a boss might protest. "A man must do a full day's work or he's no use to me." When workers tried to help themselves by forming unions, employers fought back fiercely. They didn't want anyone telling them how to run their businesses. Besides, if one worker didn't like the way things were run, the bosses figured, there was always another ready and willing to take his place.

In bad economic times bosses were firing, not hiring. And since governments had only property taxes to provide them with money, they felt both unable and unwilling to help people who were out of work.

When things went wrong, life was very hard for the working poor.

On summer nights,
some families moved
bedding outdoors to
get relief from the
heat in their small,
crowded rooms.

EMILY'S NEIGHBORHOOD

The crowded, dirty neighborhood where Emily and her family had moved was typical of the slums in the industrial cities of central and eastern North America. Whether it was Toronto, Montreal, Philadelphia, Chicago or New York, the problems were similar.

Children played on dirty streets. It could be days before a dead horse was removed.

For decades people had been flooding into the cities looking for work in the new factories. Some came from the outlying farms, but most came from European countries. Thousands of immigrants — all needing housing — poured into the cities each year. The mayors and councillors running the cities didn't know what to do about this influx. They let builders create street after street of flimsy shacks or poorly built apartment buildings, sometimes called tenements. Worst of all, there were no laws forcing builders to include running water and flush toilets.

By 1912 cities were trying to modernize. They were building sewage systems, running water pipes and stringing wires that carried electricity. Starting with public buildings such as city hall, hospitals and stores, then moving on to the well-to-do neighborhoods, the city gradually provided all with electricity and running water. The fast-growing slums were the last to receive these conveniences.

Emily's family had been forced to move into a slum. All they could afford were the two rooms that made up the ground floor of a tiny house. The upstairs rooms were rented by a family who had to climb a steep, narrow staircase on the outside of the house to reach the landing.

The Watsons used the back room for sleeping and the front room as both kitchen and parlor. They were lucky — there were only five of them. But upstairs it was a different story. Ten people lived in that tiny apartment, so some of the children had to sleep in the front room on the couch, on two chairs pushed together or on a mattress stored in the back room during the day.

One crowded room often served as both bedroom and kitchen.

Families collected water each day from a communal tap on an outdoor standpipe.

These little slum houses had no running water. Every day someone had to carry pails down the lane. Here, on a pipe sticking out of the ground, was the communal tap that drew water from the city reservoir. One family reported that the tap was forty-four steps away from their front door. Every drop of water they needed had to be carried that far once or twice a day. But they were lucky. For other families the lone neighborhood tap might be two or three streets away. People in apartment buildings sometimes had to go down five or six flights of stairs.

Because the houses had no running water, they also had no flush toilets. Most streets and lanes were lined with outdoor pit toilets, each used by two or three families. Filthy from overuse and with the stench attracting flies, they were a breeding ground for disease.

Dirt was an accepted part of life in the slums. Since water had to be carried and heated, washing floors or clothes was backbreaking work. Clothes hung to dry on lines crisscrossing back alleyways turned gray and dingy from blowing dust or the smut from coal-burning stoves. Garbage was often flung out into backyards and alleyways, attracting rats. If an animal, such as a stray dog or even an overworked horse, died, it could be months before anyone came to remove the carcass. It lay rotting on the road where children played.

IN OTHER PARTS OF THE CITY

In other parts of the city life was much better. By 1912 well-to-do families had replaced dangerous oil lamps with safe, clean electric lighting. Pipes brought water right into each house. Sewers carried away waste from sinks and from the newfangled flush toilets. Instead of pantries, where food could be kept cool for only a few days, the family now had an icebox. An ice cart delivered blocks of ice twice a week to keep the food in the icebox from spoiling. Other carts came by to pick up garbage. Men were hired to sweep the streets clean of horse droppings left when delivery wagons brought milk or vegetables or parcels from downtown shops. For the well-off, life in the city had become very pleasant.

Most of these people did not want to know how Emily and her family lived. Poor people, they reasoned, had only themselves to blame. If they worked harder they, too, would be successful. This attitude made it difficult for the mayor and councillors to use tax money to clean up the slums. But it was an attitude that would soon be challenged. Changes were coming.

Peddlers collected old clothes from well-to-do neighborhoods and sold them to papermaking factories.

CHAPTER 2

In the Factory

Emily reached for a shirtwaist from the pile in the middle of the long table. Once again she tried smiling as she caught the eye of a girl across the table. And once again she was ignored.

It wasn't as if she wanted to talk to the others, not with the constant din from the whirring sewing machines. And not after Dolly's warning. "Remember," she'd said, pointing Emily to her place at the table. "No chatting. Joe can't stand time wasters."

So there Emily had stood ever since, shoulder to shoulder with the girls on either side, part of a group of eight around the table, snipping, snipping, snipping, absolutely mute. But would it hurt to smile?

Emily sighed, then surreptitiously shifted from one foot to the other. It didn't help the dead feeling that stretched from toe to knee. "Just until the end of the summer," Mam had promised as Emily started off that morning. "I'm sure we'll hear from your father soon."

Emily lifted one foot from the floor and wiggled it about under her skirt. The end of the summer. Four months away. I've been here less than four hours and already I hate it. The numbness turned to pins and needles. Think of Mam and the little ones. What other choice was there? She put her foot down and arched her back. The girl beside her turned and glared.

A whiff of cigar smoke and a sudden snarl from behind. "What's the matter, girlie? Can't keep up with the others?"

Emily jumped. Where had he come from? "Yes, sir. I … I mean, yes, I can keep up."

"Then get on with it!"

Hands shaking, Emily spread the shirtwaist on the table in front of her. With thumb and forefinger she pulled up a thread. Be careful, she reminded herself, snipping close to the fabric.

"Faster, faster," the boss urged every time he passed that morning.

Faster? I'll snip too close. But what if he fires me because I'm too slow? The dreary thoughts were blotted out by the ache in her stomach. Oh, when will it be lunch?

The clock was on the wall behind her. She daren't turn and look again. The boss had shouted at her the first and last time she'd looked. That seemed an eternity ago, and even then her feet were numb. Now sharp pains ran across her shoulders and down her back. If she twisted her head to relieve the pain in her neck, she jostled the girl beside her, who glared silently but ferociously.

To keep from thinking about the pain, she tried figuring out the floor plan of what Dolly called "the shop." Three rows of sewing machines chattered behind her. As the sewers finished the shirtwaists, Dolly collected them to dump onto the clipping table. Then they went to the pressers farther down the room. From the corner of her eye Emily could see men sliding the blouses onto machines that hissed and belched steam into the air.

And everywhere she looked, there was Joe, badgering

this worker or that worker. She looked quickly down at her own work, afraid she might catch his eye. Sure enough, a minute later he was prowling around the clipping table, the reek of his cigar smoke making her nose twitch.

The smells in this place! Cigar smoke, the oily smell of the sewing machines, sharp whiffs of unwashed bodies and dirty clothes. And the air full of fluff. Emily no sooner had the thought than she felt a sneeze coming. A small explosion shook her. Dropping her scissors she snatched her handkerchief from her pocket and clapped it over her mouth to smother the second sneeze. She had just finished blowing the irritating fluff from her nose when she heard the boss's voice, barely audible above the clatter of sewing machines.

"That new one won't last. Too persnickety."

And then Dolly's voice. "Give her a day to get used to it."

The girl to her left had heard, too. Her dark eyes glanced sideways and met Emily's. She gave a slight toss of her head in Joe's direction, her lip curling in a quick sneer. What did that mean? Don't pay any attention? Or, that's the end of you?

A bell sounded and the sewing machines stopped. Emily still heard a roaring in her ears from the incessant din, but at last she could arch her back against the ache. The girls around her dropped their scissors into their apron pockets and headed for the row of coat hooks. Where were they going?

A gruff voice startled her. "You have lunch?" It was the girl on her left. For the first time Emily really looked at her. All morning she'd been aware only of dark, dark eyes glaring. Now she noticed the girl's face — thin, pinched, almost gaunt.

But something about the way she stood, feet planted firm, shoulders back, stopped Emily from feeling sorry for her.

"You have lunch?" The girl leaned toward Emily, all but shouting in her face.

Emily took a step back. "Yes, I have my lunch. Just over there. In my jacket."

The girl pointed to herself and said, "Magda." Then she pointed at Emily and said, "You?"

"Emily. My name is Emily Watson."

The girl nodded as though to say, So you're not so stupid after all. Then she turned and strode toward the door marked Fire Escape. Over her shoulder she said, "Come."

Emily grabbed her jacket from the row of hooks by the door and followed Magda and the other girls down a rusty iron staircase that led to an alley. Her stomach rumbled. She was starving. She sat on the lowest step and was about to reach for her lunch when she realized the girls had formed a semicircle around her. Her throat went dry.

Magda stood right in front, arms folded, glowering. "So!" The others seemed to be waiting to hear what Magda would say. "Where you work before?"

"Nowhere. This is my first —"

"You go school?"

"Yes. Yes … until last week, I —"

"You read and write good?"

"Oh, yes, I —"

Magda's scowl darkened. "Why you here? Why you take work from poor girls?"

"But I'm poor, too. We —"

"Poor! Ha! See poor girl." Magda pointed at Emily's skirt,

drawing the eyes of the other girls. "See how ripped?" Her voice dripped scorn. She pointed to Emily's laced leather boots, the ones she'd polished last night until they shone. "See hole in shoe?" She turned away with a triumphant "Ha!" The other girls scurried after her.

Emily smoothed the dark brown fabric of her skirt over her knees. What was so wrong with it? Shouldn't she look her best, going out to work for the first time? And Mam had been thrilled to discover such a fine skirt at a second-hand stall in the market. Emily looked at the retreating skirts. Faded and fraying. Some patched with mismatched cloth. Every shoe split where the leather had given way or the stitching rotted.

What could she say? She huddled closer to the step. Well, at least she could eat. The bread and cheese she had wrapped in newspaper that morning was in her jacket pocket. She shoved a hand in and her stomach lurched. With a sick taste rising in her throat, she drew out a handful of shredded paper and a few crumbs of cheese mingled with tiny black pellets. Rat droppings!

She flung the mess to the ground, as though she'd been bitten.

From farther along the alley, Magda hooted, "What you think, stupid girl? Leave lunch in pocket!"

Then Emily was alone, frantically turning her pocket inside out and shaking it as the catcalls of the girls slowly died away.

The afternoon was more of the same. By the time the finishing bell sounded at 6:15, Emily was desperate to get home. She wanted to sob out to Mam how terrible the day had been, to rant and rail about the nastiness of the girls, the throbbing of her feet, the lost lunch, the unfairness of the fate that had sent her to such a place.

She arrived at their front door sticky with sweat and the saltiness of dried tears.

"Mam!"

Hunched in a chair, eyes squinting, her mother was stitching buttons onto one of the coats Ernie had brought home. Little Bertie crawled around her feet, and baby Annie mewled in her crib. Without even looking up, Mam said, "Could you put Bertie to bed, Emmy dear? And that Ernie. I haven't seen him all day. I've got to finish these by tomorrow. I can't be late with the first batch or they mightn't give me any more."

Emily swallowed her complaints and picked up Bertie. He was sopping wet and smelly. She held him out in front, away from her good clothes, and carried him into the next room, their only bedroom. By the time she had him changed and in bed, she'd used the last drop of their water. She blinked back tears. If she once let them start, she'd never get them stopped. Four months, Mam had promised. How can I stand this for four months? And now we need water. She snatched up their two pails. The only neighborhood tap, she'd already discovered, was two streets away.

The laneway was quiet for once. The usual hordes of children must be inside having supper. But from around the corner she heard whistling. She hurried toward it.

"Ernie? Where have you been? Mam's worried sick about you."

"No she's not. She's too busy."

Emily gritted her teeth. "It's hours since school let out. What have you been doing?"

"Told you. I met some swell guys. And look what we found." Ernie waved at the small cart he'd been pushing. Their dad had made it for Ernie as a coal cart, in the days when they could still afford to buy coal.

"Where did you get that stuff?"

"Picking garbage. Rich people throw out all sorts of things. I found a lady's purse in really good shape but I traded another guy for this." Proudly he held up a large graniteware pot. "Practically new. Only one chip out of it. And look at this." From a small sack he pulled black lumps. "Coal. Just what Mam needs for the cook stove."

"Ernie, you haven't been stealing?"

"Nah! Don't have to. Told you, Em. My pal Alfie knows what's what. He can find anything. Anything! Well, gotta get home." He pushed the cart past her, whistling again.

Emily sighed and picked up the pails. They needed water. And no matter where Ernie had got it, they now had a bit of coal to add to their meager fuel supply. But garbage picking. Her brother reduced to garbage picking?

She clenched her teeth. I can't think about this. I just can't. In a few hours I have to get up and go back to that dreadful place.

Just get the water, she told herself. And then she remembered the one comfort she had to look forward to. On the back of the stove, simmering gently, was the soup she and Mam had made yesterday — beans and cabbage with a scattering of carrots and their last potato. Waiting.

~

For the next few days the girls worked beside Emily in hostile silence. At lunchtime, when they all gathered on the fire-escape stairs, they pointedly shifted away from the step she chose, chattering in a language she didn't recognize. But she'd learned from them. Now her lunch was packed in a small tin pail — ratproof — just like the ones she'd noticed them carrying. Even this didn't lessen their contempt.

The morning of the fourth day she hung her jacket on a peg in a sleepwalking trance and trailed after the other girls to their table. Something was different this morning. Emily shook herself awake. The girls were usually so silent. Today they seemed restless. The girl who stood across from her — Katya, Emily had heard her called — was coughing blood into her handkerchief as usual. Along the table other girls sniffled or squinted through red-rimmed eyes at the threads they were trimming. One girl had a huge festering sore on her cheek. What a sickly lot we are, Emily thought.

Caught up in her thoughts, Emily reached automatically for a shirtwaist from the waiting pile. Then she realized what was different. Magda wasn't beside her. She half turned and spotted her standing by the row of coat hooks. No, Magda was leaning against the wall, her head resting on her jacket. How strange! At the sound of the starting bell Magda pushed herself upright and walked slowly toward the table.

Asleep on her feet, like the rest of us, Emily thought. She glanced sideways, but Magda seemed to have perked up. She had her scissors out and a shirtwaist spread in front of her. Just get on with your own work, Emily told herself, squaring her shoulders and planting her feet firmly. She had soon learned that if she stood up straight with her feet apart, the pains in her legs and back didn't start until much later in the morning. She was snipping energetically when Magda jostled her arm, almost making Emily drive the points of her scissors into the fabric.

"Sorry, sorry." The words sounded slurred. Emily looked sharply at Magda, but the girl had her head down, working intently. With a start Emily realized the boss was behind them. The smell of cigar smoke gave him away. She'd learned the hard way that both he and Dolly could creep up soundlessly on their rubber-soled shoes.

"What's this?" he snatched up Magda's shirtwaist and

pointed to the bottom edge. A tiny hole showed where Magda's scissors had cut too close to the fabric. "That's two cents off you, girlie. And don't let it happen again today or it'll be four cents the next time."

Magda stared at the floor, her hands kneading her apron. Emily stared in astonishment. The nick was barely visible! And it was in the bottom hem. Who would notice? She opened her mouth to protest, but as Joe's eyes swung round the table, she swallowed the words. What were Magda's problems to her, after all? She had worries of her own.

Out of the corner of her eye, Emily saw Joe ball up Magda's shirtwaist and toss it at Dolly. Surely she wouldn't throw it out. Mam would just turn the hem up another bit to hide the cut. And why be so nasty about it? Everyone worked hard. From starting bell to ending bell, there was not one idle hand anywhere the whole length of the room. At the end of each day Dolly had dozens of neatly hemmed and pressed shirtwaists to pack into the boxes stacked beside the fire-escape door. He should be grateful.

Emily was startled out of her thoughts by something jostling her arm. She heard a thud and turned to see Magda slumped on the floor. Throwing down her work, Emily knelt and put a hand on Magda's forehead.

"She's burning up," Emily said as Dolly arrived. "She must have a fever."

"No, no." Magda's eyes flickered open. "I good ... good." She struggled to sit up. "I okay work."

"Sure you are, kid. Upsy-daisy." Dolly put a hand under Magda's arm, and together she and Emily hoisted Magda to her feet. As Magda gripped the table, swaying, Emily caught sight of the girls across from them. White-faced and staring. Not one had moved as the little drama unfolded.

"What's going on here? Anybody's messed up those shirts, I'll —"

"Calm down, Joe. The shirts are fine." With her arm still around a shaky Magda, Dolly turned to the boss. "Let the girl sit down for a minute. We need to get everyone else back to work if we're going to make our quota."

"Sit down?" The sudden bark made Emily jump. She could see the veins standing out on Joe's forehead as he chewed furiously on his cigar. "Stupid girl. Holding up production. Ah, what else can you expect from a dumb Polack."

Emily whirled on the foreman. How dare he! Inside her head she was screaming, She's one of your best workers! But before the hot words could spill out, Dolly was in front of her.

"Button your lip," she hissed. "And get back to work."

Emily felt her mouth snap shut. She turned back to the table and saw a ring of shocked eyes. Her knees started to shake. What if he fired me? And Mam without one cent in her purse?

"Get on with your work, the lot of you," Joe snarled as Emily picked up her scissors. For a long moment she felt him hovering. Then, in an angry cloud of cigar smoke, he moved on.

Snip. Snip. Snip. Don't think. Just work. Slowly the trembling calmed. She had finished four more shirtwaists when she realized Magda was back beside her. She daren't so much as turn her head. Who knew where the boss might be, prowling on silent rubber soles? A few minutes later, through the noise of the sewing machines, she heard a whisper from beside her.

"T'anks for help Magda. Nice girl."

GARMENT FACTORY GIRLS

Emily was one of thousands of young girls working in garment factories in the big cities of North America. These factories produced inexpensive clothing for the ever-growing hordes of workers flocking to the cities' offices and factories.

Until the mid-nineteenth century, clothes had been made mostly in the home, one garment at a time, sized to fit a particular family member. The invention of the sewing machine in 1845 changed all that. The time it took to produce clothes was reduced dramatically.

The factory system cut the time and the cost even more. Each factory specialized: one might make men's coats, another trousers or men's ties. The small factory Emily worked in made a type of women's blouse called a shirtwaist. Because factories made the same garment over and over, the owners could buy fabric in large quantities. This meant they paid less for it than someone buying small amounts.

To keep costs down even more, factory owners hired workers with few skills. They preferred female workers, especially teenaged girls and children. Their small hands and nimble fingers were good for working with intricate machinery.

Many workers were legally too young to work. If the factory owners were caught, they might have to pay a fine. Often, however, they could bribe an inspector to look the other way. The money they saved by hiring cheap labor made the risk worth their while.

Because of the long hours, low wages and unhealthy conditions, these factories were called "sweatshops." The workers earned their tiny wages "by the sweat of their brow."

Girls as young as ten worked in garment factories.

IN THE FACTORY

The factory was a fast and efficient way to produce clothing because the making of each garment was divided into many small tasks. This "task system" allowed the factory owners to hire unskilled girls who could quickly be taught the one task they would perform over and over again. As well as many unskilled workers, a typical garment factory also had some skilled workers.

THE FLOOR BOSS

The owner of a small factory like the one where Emily worked, with just a few dozen workers, was also the floor boss. He oversaw all the steps needed to create the finished product. He bought the fabric, hired the workers and sold the finished goods to store owners. Owners of large factories (with 500 or more workers) hired floor bosses to run their factories.

The floor boss supervised dozens of seamstresses in this large factory.

THE FORELADY

The forelady (or in a large factory, the foreman) supervised the workers. She decided how much work each person would do each day (called their "stint"). She also checked that the garments met factory standards — the stitches were even and the seams straight. The forelady kept the partially sewn garments moving along the assembly line so that the next worker could do her part with no delays.

THE DRAPER

The draper might be either a man or a woman. It was the draper's job to turn a design drawn on paper into a pattern that could be used to cut out the different parts of a garment. To do this he took a long piece of muslin (a thin cotton fabric) and draped it around a tailor's dummy. Then he pinned and cut and shaped it into a blouse, skirt or other garment. Finally a pattern was created for the cutters. Drapers were skilled workers who could earn high wages.

THE CUTTERS

The cutters were always men. They stacked up to twenty-four layers of fabric on long tables, laid the pattern pieces on top and cut them with razor-sharp knives. To avoid wasting fabric, cutters learned to lay out the pattern pieces as tightly as the pieces of a jigsaw puzzle. They also had to be strong enough to cut quickly and accurately through all the layers at once. Skilled cutters were paid the top wages in garment factories.

THE SEAMSTRESSES

The sewing machine operators, almost all teenaged girls or young women, sat at tables arranged in long rows. Each seamstress would sew only one part of the garment, maybe the side seams or the sleeves. It took ten seamstresses to finish one shirtwaist blouse. The pace was set by the fastest sewer and everyone was badgered to keep up with her. Repeating the same action over and over made the job tedious and tiring.

THE CLIPPING GIRLS

The finished garment had dozens of threads hanging from it. The threads had to be clipped with care so that the garment would not be ruined, a task easily taught to young girls. Unskilled and usually underage, these girls were very poorly paid. Emily started out as a clipper in her factory.

THE PRESSERS

The steam irons were too heavy for girls. The pressers were men who stood at rows of ironing boards pressing the finished garments. The gas-fired irons hissed steam into the air, making that part of the room damp and humid in all weather. Once pressed, the garments were carefully folded and packed, ready to be delivered to stores.

Overhead pipes delivered steam from a boiler to the heavy irons used by the pressers.

SHIRTWAIST AND SKIRT: THE WORKING GIRL'S UNIFORM

The factory where Emily and Magda worked made a type of woman's blouse called a shirtwaist. By 1912, all over North America, hundreds of small factories were making shirtwaists. As more and more women worked outside the home, they demanded clothing that was simple and easy to care for. The shirtwaist, with its neat, tailored look, was the perfect solution.

Many shirtwaists were cotton, usually white, with long sleeves and pleated fronts. They were easy to wash and iron, so that working women could always appear neat and clean. Some women wore a man's tie to give themselves a more businesslike appearance. Shirtwaists were worn with ankle-length skirts. Because their skirts no longer swept the ground, women and girls could move more energetically as they left their homes for school or work. They could also take part in such sports as tennis, bicycling and boating.

Shirtwaists came in various styles and materials, from lace-trimmed silk for wealthy customers to plain white cotton for working girls and women.

HOUSEMAID: A FATE WORSE THAN FACTORY WORKER

Factories were both good and bad. Even though the working conditions were almost always uncomfortable and dangerous, factories offered some advantages over working as a housemaid, the only other job available to unskilled city girls.

Housemaids lived in tiny attic rooms in their employers' houses. They were up before dawn, lugging coal or wood from the cellar to kindle fires. During the day they worked hard scrubbing floors and doing other heavy household chores. They also washed and ironed clothes and helped to prepare meals. Long after dark, when they finally finished washing the last of the dirty pots and pans and had tidied up the kitchen, they could finally go to bed, only to be up a few hours later to begin again.

Employers allowed their maids one half day off, every second week, often insisting this be spent in church. Many employers strongly discouraged "walking out" (having a boyfriend). If a housemaid was seen talking to a young man, she might be "turned off without a character" (fired without a letter of reference for the next employer). By comparison factory girls had the freedom to do as they pleased with what little spare time they had.

Scouring pots was one of many dirty jobs done by housemaids.

HOME WORK

Emily's mother needed to earn money, but with a baby and a toddler to look after, she was not free to go out to work. Her solution was to work at home doing "piecework." This meant she was paid a few pennies for each piece she finished. Mrs. Watson's job was to sew buttons on coats. Other pieceworkers might baste seams, sew in linings or stitch hems. Young children could earn a few pennies by pulling basting threads.

Home workers supplied their own thread and, if necessary, their own sewing machines. Sitting around the kitchen table, young mothers, the elderly and any children old enough to help labored together hour after hour. Most had to work all day and well into the night to finish enough pieces to make even a pittance.

Sewing wasn't the only type of piecework farmed out to home workers. Some families made flowers for ladies' hats by gluing tiny petals to wire stems. Others strung beads, rolled cigarettes or cigars, pushed bristles into hairbrushes or sewed up powder puffs.

To get supplies the family sent a child, often a boy of ten or twelve, to act as the runner between home and factory. At the beginning of the day or week he collected whatever materials were needed for the family's piecework. At the end of the day or week he took the finished products back to the factory.

The factories that used home workers were small. They were run out of tenement apartments or rented basement rooms where the contractor and a few workers finished assembling and packing the garments or other products made by the home workers.

Even the youngest children in a family helped with piecework.

OTHER FACTORIES WHERE CHILDREN WORKED

Children were hired to work in many different kinds of factories. With machines doing the heavy work that once had been done by men, employers found that children could be hired at less than half the adult wages. This had two unfortunate consequences. Children were taken out of school early and never learned skills that would help them get better jobs. And hiring children took jobs away from adults, so more and more families had to rely on the wages of their children.

TEXTILE MILLS

Girls as young as ten were hired to tend the bobbins (cylinders on which yarn was wound). If a thread broke, they had to quickly tie the ends together. After fourteen hours a day of running up and down six or eight long rows of machinery, tending the whirling bobbins, a girl would go home with sore eyes, an aching back, throbbing legs and swollen feet. Boys worked as "doffers," replacing full bobbins with empty ones. They worked barefoot to make it easier to climb up the machinery to reach the top rows of bobbins. It also brought them dangerously close to whirling machinery. As a result, many lost fingers and toes.

Bare feet made it easier for boys to climb on the spinning frames to replace the bobbins, but it was dangerous work.

GLASS FACTORIES

Young boys worked in the furnace rooms, assisting the glassblowers. Because of the heat and the glare from the fire, the boys suffered from headaches, heat exhaustion and burns, as well as cuts from the broken glass that littered the floor. The furnaces were never turned off, so many of the boys had to work all night.

The floor boss taught child workers how to run the machinery.

In glass factories, intense heat from the furnaces made working conditions unpleasant.

CANNERIES

Canning season was short and frantic. As the freshly picked beans, corn or tomatoes arrived at the canneries, children as young as seven or eight cut and chopped and husked for twelve hours a day. At seaside canneries, shucking oysters and peeling shrimp left them with swollen and bleeding fingers. Once the short season was over they were out of work.

In canneries, children as young as eight were expected to place lids on cans at the rate of forty a minute.

A boy makes melon baskets in a basket factory.

BISCUIT AND OTHER FACTORIES

No matter what a factory produced — matches, cigars, biscuits — each person on the assembly line endlessly repeated one small task. In a biscuit factory biscuits streamed along a conveyor belt. Girls would dab each one with a teaspoon of jam, then, farther down the line, other girls would place a biscuit on top of each to make a sandwich. Finally the finished biscuits were packed into small cardboard boxes. The endless repetition made the job boring and exhausting.

COAL MINES

Young boys were hired for many dangerous yet tedious jobs. Ten-year-olds cleaned and sorted the coal. For twelve hours a day they bent over streams of coal pouring out of chutes, reaching into the fast-moving, sharp-edged coal to pick out slate and stones. Older boys tended doors in dark mine tunnels. When they heard the rumble of approaching coal carts, they had to pull open the heavy doors, then leap out of the way as the large carts rushed through. Others controlled the speed of rolling carts by jamming wooden sticks into the wheels to brake them. Many lost fingers, hands or legs at these dangerous jobs. Most had chronic bronchitis from inhaling clouds of coal dust.

Filthy from coal dust, this boy has just finished a twelve-hour shift.

47

CHAPTER 3

Payday

Emily stared at Magda's broad back as they inched forward
in line. She could hear excited whispering behind her and
felt her own spirits soar. Payday! Four whole dollars in the
little brown envelope with her name on it.

And how they needed it. But even though most of it
would go for rent, Mam had said, "Stop at the bakery on
your way home. See if they have any day-old bread. And
maybe a little meat pie. As a treat."

"Move along, now." Dolly was standing beside the
front door ticking off names in a ledger. "Shapiro, Colletti,
Manofsky …" Beside her, Joe handed out small brown
envelopes. The seamstresses went first, then the pressers.
Finally the clipping girls shuffled by.

Just two more. Emily brushed her sleeve over her damp
forehead, then glanced at the clock. Five past four. Hurry,
hurry, or the bakeshop will be out of meat pies. Saturday,
their short day, was the only day she had even a hope of
finding bargains at the bakery.

"Altman … Takacs …" That was Magda. At last. Now me.
She heard a gasp, and Magda stopped so abruptly that Emily
walked right into her.

The problem seemed to be the girl ahead of Magda —
Sonia. She had her pay envelope upside down and was

shaking it frantically. "Nothing?" Her voice rose to a hysterical wail. "Nothing!"

"Keep moving," Dolly's voice cut in sharply. "Takacs. Watson."

The excited whispering behind Emily had stopped.

"Move along," Dolly said again. Magda held out her hand for her envelope, then shoved it into her pocket.

"What's —?" Emily had one hand on Magda's sleeve.

"Shh!" Magda hissed sharply. She hurried over to Sonia who stood sobbing just outside the door. With an arm around her shoulders Magda urged her toward the stairs.

Emily held out her hand automatically, her eyes still on the scene on the landing. But as she closed her fingers over the envelope, she felt the outline of coins, and her heart jumped with relief.

She ran down the dark stairs and out the door to find Magda waiting alone. Some way up the lane Emily could see the girl with the empty pay packet walking with friends. They huddled around her, moving slowly, like a funeral procession.

"Sonia had nothing," Emily burst out. "Not one cent!" Yes, she'd heard Joe docking various of the workers — two cents here, five cents there — for being too long in the washroom, losing a spool of thread, spoiling a piece of lace edging. But four whole dollars! "That's just not fair. How can he do that?"

Magda shrugged, tight-lipped. "Boss make rules. For us, is nothing can do." She gestured with her head. "You come?"

Emily sighed and fell in beside Magda. Was it true? That nothing could be done? They all worked hard. Why should spending a minute too long in the washroom … What had

Miss Henderson said about the dignity of labor?

A voice broke into her thoughts. Magda was looking at her expectantly. "Pardon?"

Magda's cheeks reddened. "You bring — you know?" She gave a little shrug.

"Oh yes, of course." Emily reached into her pocket and pulled out a carefully folded page from a tattered newspaper she'd found blowing down the street. Magda reached for it eagerly, running her finger under the sentence Emily pointed to.

"Last evening …" Magda sounded out the words carefully, "… at the lah … lah …"

"Labor Temple," Emily said. "You know — that big building where we turn on Main Street."

"Lay – burr – Temple," Magda repeated, "… this reporter … atten … ded a … meeting …"

Emily's thoughts drifted back to last Wednesday. She and Magda had been staring into the candy store window. How long had it been since she'd had money for treats? To tantalize herself she'd been reading down the list of sweets when Magda burst out, "You read good." Then, in a quick mumble, "You teach Magda?" They'd been working at it for a week now, in the fifteen minutes they shared on the walk home, and Emily had quickly realized that Magda knew how to read. It was English she needed to learn.

"What mean this?" Magda was running her finger under the next sentence.

"… garment workers currently on strike …" Emily read out, then, "Wait a minute. Let me see that?" She glanced quickly down the article, then read out loud, "Young female garment workers are currently on strike against the Bijou Shirtwaist and Vesture Company, which operates a walkup factory in this city. The featured speaker, Mrs. Cornelius van der Heyden, a renowned crusader for the rights of working women, told a crowd of 150, 'We are here to protest against the wrongs that have caused these poor women and girls to strike against this heartless company — the crowded, filthy working conditions, the long hours of toil, the meager pittance on which they are forced to live, barely enough to provide subsistence living in this city. All so that the cold-hearted factory proprietors can make a few more pennies of profit. These girls are no older than the daughters of many of us here, and yet they are brave enough to strike a blow against this grave injustice.'"

Emily could feel her heart racing. "They're writing about us, Magda. Somewhere in this city girls just like us are —"

"No read this." Magda almost snatched the paper out of Emily's hand.

"What do you mean? This is important. It could help us —"

"No! Boss … boss …" Her face contorted with the effort of making herself understood.

"He can't stop us from talking," Emily started, but the agitated look on Magda's face stopped her. "Never mind," she said quickly. "Here. Try this sentence." She pointed to a headline about a fly-swatting contest. Rid Our City of Flies. That seemed safe enough.

Magda took the paper with shaking hands, but she made no attempt to read. She walked on, taking deep breaths. They had covered almost a whole block before she started sounding out words.

Emily watched her, warily. To be that upset about something in a newspaper. To be afraid even to think about protesting. Why, I would never ... Emily stopped in mid-thought. Never what? Never let Joe scare me? She patted the little brown envelope tucked safely into her skirt pocket. That's the reason we're all scared. But somewhere in this city, she realized again with amazement, somewhere there are factory girls who aren't afraid. How can that be?

By the time they reached the corner where they went different ways, Magda had managed to sound out four sentences.

"You're doing very well," Emily said and was glad to see a small, answering smile.

"See ... you ... to ... morrow," Magda shaped the words carefully, just as Emily had taught her. She waved as she headed away.

I'll miss Magda, Emily thought in surprise, as she set off toward the bakery near her own street. As soon as Dad ... If Dad ... No, don't think that way.

She let herself be caught up in the street hustle and bustle. Pushcart sellers sang out their wares: "Peanuts, getcher peanuts!" or "Shoelaces!" or "Needles and thread!" The organ-grinder added the raucous wheeze of his hurdy-gurdy to the hubbub as his monkey reached for pennies from the shrieking crowd of children. And all around her strolled people clutching their precious pay packets. Emily felt her spirits rise — it was almost like a party.

Up ahead she could see shoppers bustling in and out of the bakery. She had just reached the door when she heard Ernie calling.

"Wait up, Em!" Bent double under a heavy load of coats for Mam to finish, he elbowed his way through the crowd.

"Guess what?" He stopped to catch his breath. "That stuff me 'n' Alfie found? Rag 'n' bone man gave me a dime for it. A dime, Em!"

"That's wonderful, Ernie." Emily glanced through the bakeshop window. An empty bread basket, two empty cake plates. She felt a pang of disappointment.

Ernie prattled on. "Now me 'n' Alf can buy some newspapers and sell 'em downtown. Alf knows the best corner. Kids get rich selling papers, y'know. Soon's me and Alf gets set up in the newspaper business, Mam won't have to bother with … You listening, Em?"

"Look, Ernie!" She pointed to a plate in a dark corner. "Meat pies. Maybe that was a lucky dime you earned today."

As the weeks passed Emily kept her eyes open. Every payday someone was short. This isn't right, she thought. We need every penny we earn, just like the newspaper said.

Magda refused to talk about it. "Boss make rules," she kept repeating.

Maybe she's right. Emily had read through the whole newspaper article several times, and she still couldn't see how someone up on a platform talking about "striking a blow against injustice" was going to help her or Magda or Katya. And besides, she told herself, when Dad gets home ... But that thought led to a panicky flutter in her stomach. Please let him come home soon. Please let this job be just for the summer.

The days dragged on, hot and tiring and long. But not quite unbearable. Ernie often had leftover papers. The newspaper business wasn't as easy as he'd expected. And Emily found she enjoyed reading the papers with Magda, hearing her English improve day by day.

Could I be a teacher, she wondered, like Miss Henderson? No, maybe that was asking too much. Just let me go to Continuation School, and I'll be content.

They'd started reading on the way to work as well as on the way home, so Emily was puzzled one particularly hot morning when there was no Magda waiting for her. She hurried on, glancing back every so often, just in case Magda was late. By the time she turned into Mill Lane she was running. The group of clipping girls was ahead of her, already opening the factory door.

"Katya?" she called. "Where's Magda?"

Katya shook her head and shrugged. Emily turned to the others, but they were already quietly filing up the stairs. Didn't they care? Something must have happened. Magda came even when she was sick.

Upstairs, Dolly's "Where's Magda?" was met with shrugs and head shakings. She turned to Emily.

"I waited at the corner as long as I could." And then Emily saw Joe bearing down on them.

"That's her finished, then," he growled when Dolly explained. "There's lots more out there waiting."

Emily heard quick gasps around the table. But Dolly stepped in front of Joe as he turned to go.

"Now wait a minute, Joe. She's a good worker. And she trains the other girls for me. Let's just give her a day. Find out what's happened."

"One day, then. If she's not back tomorrow, that's it."

Dolly tightened her lips as Joe stamped off. She shifted the load of shirtwaists in her arms and looked around the table of staring girls. "Someone tell Magda what Joe said. Make sure she's here tomorrow."

Emily was amazed to see the other girls look away from Dolly, their faces blank. Weren't they supposed to be Magda's friends? "I'll do it," she heard herself say.

Dolly nodded. "Tell her she's lucky Joe's giving her one more chance. If she's back tomorrow, there'll be nothing more said and only one day's pay docked."

Later that day, as the closing bell sounded, Emily turned to Katya. "Show me where Magda lives," she said. "We have to make sure she's back tomorrow."

All the clipping girls started off in a group, but one by one the others slipped down side streets and were gone. Katya's eyes followed them longingly, but Emily held her hand tightly. "Take me to Magda," she said firmly, and Katya walked on obediently.

Once they'd turned the corner where she usually left Magda, Emily could feel the neighborhood change. Instead of houses, apartment buildings loomed over the narrow street, shutting out the sun. Along the curbs and in the gutters scrawny, ragged children crouched, using pebbles to play marbles. Somewhere close by, Emily could hear the roar of a train. The air was gritty with dirt and dust from its cinder-belching engine.

Katya turned into a side street, then, with an anxious glance at Emily, down a narrow alleyway between two apartments. The stench of overflowing privies filled Emily's nostrils. She began breathing through her mouth. This was even worse than the smell in their own lane.

They came out of the dark into a patch of light. There was a tiny yard filled with debris — a legless chair, a wheel from a cart, a mattress sodden with something that gave off an acrid smell, a jumble of rusting iron rods. Surrounding the yard squatted the dirty brick walls of four apartments. Clotheslines crisscrossed from window to window. High up, a woman was leaning out to take in laundry.

"Magda there." Katya pointed to what appeared to be cellar steps leading down to a small landing. Then she turned and darted away.

At the bottom of the steps, beside the door, flies buzzed around a bucket that gave off a fetid smell. Emily's stomach heaved. I can't, she thought, and turned to follow Katya down the alley. But what if Magda was fired? Get it over with, she told herself and hurried down the crumbling cement stairs, holding her breath as she knocked on the door. It opened a crack, and a small girl of about six or seven, sucking vigorously on one finger, stared up at her.

"Magda? Is she here?" Emily asked.

The girl opened the door wider and moved aside, still sucking at her finger.

Emily stepped into a dank chilliness that made her shiver. Suddenly Magda was in front of her.

"You? Why you come?"

"Dolly sent me." Magda's stone-faced stare made Emily hurry on. "She said if you're back tomorrow, you'll still have your job." Then, as Magda said nothing, "What happened? Why did you miss today?"

Magda looked down at her clenched hands and stepped back. Behind her, on a bench along the wall, sat three more little girls, their dark eyes regarding Emily gravely.

Magda waved toward a dark corner where, on the floor, Emily could see the pale outlines of what might be a mattress. A harsh, croaking cough came from the small figure huddled there.

"Sister too sick. Must stay."

"But your mother …"

"No mother. Papa out all day."

"What can I do? Can I help?" Emily glanced around. A table that was no more than a wide board resting on packing cases took up most of the center of the small room. A piece of ancient but well-scrubbed linoleum covered the bare wood floor in front of an unlit cook stove. "Food …?"

But Magda was edging her toward the door. "I back tomorrow," she said. She opened the door and all but pushed Emily out onto the landing beside the stinking chamber pot. The door closed with a sharp click, and Emily felt a flicker of annoyance. It had taken some effort, after all, to get here. Holding a hand over her nose, trying not to breath in the foul smell, she ran up the stairs and along the alley. Well, she'd delivered the message. That was as much as she could do.

Out on the street she gulped down fresher air. Mam would be wondering where she was. She thought of Mam's ever-simmering soup pot, and her stomach rumbled. What were those children going to eat? There'd been no sign of supper underway in that bleak room. No mother, Magda had said. So who looked after the children all day? She thought about Annie and Bertie. Without Mam ...? Emily shivered in the heat of the July evening.

The next morning Emily slowed down as she approached Magda's corner. No one was waiting. What if I have to tell Dolly? Well, what can I say? I delivered the message.

Then she was at the corner and there, trudging up the side street, was the familiar stocky figure. Relief surged through Emily. There must be good news about the little sister. She smiled expectantly, but Magda just turned and walked beside her in silence. Remembering the look Magda had given her yesterday, Emily thought, No. Better not to ask.

True to her word, Dolly said nothing once Magda was back in her place. And on Saturday Magda's brown envelope was short one day's pay.

"You should have told them why," Emily said on the way home.

But Magda just shrugged.

Emily ground her teeth. Magda and her "Boss make rules" was becoming infuriating. But to be fair, it was really Joe's fault.

That newspaper article had said that some girls were standing up to their bosses. So why couldn't the girls at the Acme factory do the same? Why couldn't Magda just tell Joe why she'd missed a day? But by Sunday noon, as she sat in their front room, spooning milk-soaked bread into Bertie's eager mouth, Emily knew the answer. Just yesterday the rent collector had taken the last dollar in Mam's purse. Unless Ernie sold more papers than usual, they had only a few pennies left until Emily's next pay packet. Without that money could they end up in a cellar room like Magda's?

The scraping of Ernie's chair broke into her thoughts. He was on his feet, wiping his mouth with the back of one hand, and shoving away his empty porridge bowl with the other. "I'm off," he said. "Me 'n' Alf's got important stuff to do."

"Empty that chamber pot first. You should have done it ages ago."

"Not me! That's girl's work." Ernie darted around the table, brushing Mam's sewing onto the floor.

He'd be gone in a second. Emily snatched up the chamber pot and thrust it at him. "Mam said … "

But he already had the door open. The sloshing contents of the pot slowed her down. By the time she'd clamped one hand over the lid and skirted the table, he was out. She launched herself through the doorway screaming, "Ernie, you get — !" and choked on the next word.

There, standing in the lane, her elegant skirt held up

and away from the trash littering the pathway, was Miss Henderson. Emily felt her face flame. To be caught holding a stinking chamber pot and screaming like a fishwife.

"May I come in, Emily?"

Emily had a quick vision of their tiny, cluttered front room. She swallowed and backed through the doorway. "Yes, yes, of course. Please …" She ducked quickly to shove the chamber pot behind the stove.

Bertie was beating his spoon on the tray of his highchair. Just then Mam came out of the bedroom with baby Annie in her arms. "Emily, what on earth …?" She stopped short as she took in the visitor. "Oh." Her face went blank. "Miss Henderson."

"I'm so sorry to come unannounced, Mrs. Watson." Emily could see a flush of embarrassment on her teacher's face. "I went back to your old address hoping to find Emily, and your neighbor sent me on here."

"Yes, of course," Mam said with a bewildered look at Emily, who rushed to pull a chair away from the table.

"Please sit down." Emily scooped the pile of Mam's factory sewing off the seat. What on earth must Miss Henderson think of them?

"Put the kettle on for tea, Emily." Mam's voice was calm again. In control. It will be a pale cup, Emily thought, picturing how little tea was left in the canister.

Still standing just inside the door, Miss Henderson put out one gloved hand. "No, please, nothing. I'll only stay a minute, Mrs. Watson. I promised Emily …" She reached for a stiff, white envelope tucked under her arm. "I have your graduation certificate, my dear. The principal agreed with me that, even though you didn't write the final examinations, you deserve to get credit for the splendid work you did this year."

Emily rubbed her hands down her apron front, then reached for the envelope. "Emily Watson," it said in Miss Henderson's bold calligraphy. She found she was holding her breath as she slid out a white certificate.

"Withrow Public School … Senior Fourth Leaving Certificate … Emily Watson … With distinction …"

She felt Mam's hand on her shoulder. "Oh, Emmy. How wonderful!"

Emily looked at her teacher and had to swallow before she could whisper, "Thank you."

Miss Henderson reached for her hand. "Remember, Emily. This is your key to the future. I promise you …" The teacher stopped and her eyes darted around the shabby little room. "Even if things seem bleak now, there will come a day when this will help you get the job you deserve."

Emily opened her mouth. What could she say? She felt overwhelmed by all the hopes she'd had. She wanted so badly to beg, "Please take me away from here." The effort to keep back those shaming words left her tongue-tied.

Mam rushed to fill the silence. "Thank you for coming, Miss Henderson. We appreciate … I always wanted Emily to finish school, but as you can see …" Mam pinched her lips together.

Miss Henderson nodded. What did that look mean? Was it sympathy or pity? Before Emily could decide, the teacher had turned back to her. "Don't ever give up hope, Emily." Hope, there was that word again. By the time Emily had collected her thoughts the door had closed behind her teacher.

Bertie banged on his chair tray and let out a cranky yelp. Emily picked up the sodden lump he'd dropped on the floor and popped it into his mouth as Mam turned back from the door.

"Let me see the certificate again, Emmy." Mam put Annie into her cradle before taking the certificate carefully by the corners. "With distinction." She repeated the words reverently. "It's a dream come true. You know, Emmy, that I …? Well, that's all water under the bridge now. The important thing is, here you are with a school leaving certificate."

Emily watched her mother almost drinking in the words — words that proved to the world that she, Emily Watson, had been to school. But what if she'd had to leave school when she was only nine, like her mother? What if she'd had to spend three years at home looking after the little ones, like her mother? At least I've had this much more, she thought. Mam made sure of that.

"Here, take it before it gets soiled. Tuck it into the Bible. We must keep it safe." Mam's eyes filled with tears. "I'm so proud of you, Emmy. And when your father gets home …"

But that was one hope too many for Emily. Suddenly she couldn't keep the words back any longer. "What if he doesn't come back? What will we do then?"

Her mother's face went white. "No, Emily, we mustn't think like that. Your father would never … He has never let me down. We knew going out west was a risk. But he would never just abandon us. Never." She took Emily's face between her two hands. "You must believe that, Emily. As I do. The minute he can, he'll be in touch."

Emily swallowed the rest of her hot words. How could

she argue when Mam needed so badly to believe?

"Now tuck your certificate away safely."

Obediently, Emily turned toward the bedroom. Mam's Bible was in the battered trunk that held their few spare clothes. Emily lifted the lid, then looked once more at the certificate — Mam's dream come true. But not even the words "Graduated with distinction" could dissolve the sick feeling in Emily's stomach.

Because it's all gone wrong, she thought. Somehow Mam's dream just hasn't worked out.

EMILY'S PAY PACKET

Emily was paid four dollars a week for sixty hours of work. Her family had almost no other money they could count on, so Emily's pay packet had to support five people.

In 1912 prices for food and clothing were very low compared to today. Even so, a well-off family expected to spend twelve dollars a week for rent, food and fuel for cooking, heating and lighting. With Emily's pay plus the small amount Mrs. Watson and Ernie could bring in — perhaps another two dollars if they were lucky — Emily's family had less than half that amount.

Rent took two dollars every week. That left three dollars (occasionally four dollars) to pay for food and fuel. With the cheapest cuts of meat costing from ten to eighteen cents a pound and eggs thirty-three cents a dozen, the Watsons had to live on potatoes, beans and day-old bread.

For heating and cooking, well-off families spent thirty-five cents a week on bituminous coal, the cheapest kind. Poor families sent their children out to scavenge for bits of coal and wood in the hopes of not having to buy it. But they did have to spend twenty-four cents a week for the coal oil necessary to light at least one lamp so that there was light for sewing piecework to earn money.

Even in better times Mrs. Watson had bought their clothing at the secondhand stalls or made clothing for the younger children out of hand-me-downs. Now she had to mend their clothes until everything was patched, or search among the clothes donated to charity organizations. Mrs. Watson had always had to budget carefully. Now even the best budgeting would barely cover rent, food and clothing for her family.

(left) Boys often spent their spare time at the dump, hoping to find bits of copper, paper and rags to sell.

(right) This girl is on her way home with a bag of scavenged coal.

Main Street: 1912

Emily and Ernie were used to city streets bustling with activity and noise. Many vendors who could not afford to rent stores sold their goods from pushcarts. The streets rang with their cries, "Needles!" "Ribbons!" "Hot peanuts!" Newsboys shouted the latest headlines, horses clip-clopped by on iron-shod feet and the whole cacophony was punctuated by the clang of streetcar bells or a honk from one of the few cars or trucks around.

Over it all hung a miasma of smells: roasting nuts, garlicky pickles and fresh-baked bread mingled with the stench of horse droppings. Even though cleaners swept tons of droppings off the streets, pedestrians had to watch carefully where they stepped. Strolling main street in 1912 was an adventure.

(above) Pushcart vendors had to watch out for boys trying to steal their wares.

(right) The business streets in cities were often clogged with street vendors.

THE IMMIGRANTS

The oldest child babysat her younger siblings.

Emily was amazed to discover that the other girls working around the clipping table spoke almost no English. Even though Emily and the children she went to school with were the children of immigrants, their parents had all come from England, Ireland or Scotland. They blended very easily into their new country. But in the new neighborhood, and especially in the factory, Emily felt as though she had entered a strange and unsettling world.

She wasn't the only one who felt out of place. Magda, Katya and the other girls knew exactly how strange it was to leave the country of their birth and travel to a place where everything was different, often frightening and always difficult.

Magda and her family were part of the enormous migration from eastern and southern Europe that had been going on since about 1880. In countries such as Russia, Galicia (now part of Ukraine and Poland), Poland, Lithuania, Italy and Greece, many people were out of work. They also had other worries. As their sons reached sixteen, they looked for ways to save them from service in armies that seemed always to need more and more soldiers for the endless wars that plagued Europe. Some groups in eastern Europe, such as Jews and Mennonites, were under attack because of their religion. Letters from friends and relatives in North America told of freedom from all these troubles. Better still, they told of a world where even the poorest could eat meat every day. If a poor person could buy meat, some reasoned, maybe the rumors were true — maybe the streets in this new world really were paved with gold.

Getting to North America was difficult. The cheapest fares were ten dollars a person — an enormous amount of money when almost every penny earned went to feed, clothe and house their family. To raise the money most had to sell their most valuable possession, often the family cow. Even so, many could afford to send only one or two family members. Usually the father and oldest child went first. They planned to work in their new country until they had saved enough money to bring the rest of the family.

The journey by ship was three weeks of misery. The ten-dollar fare provided each immigrant with nothing but a berth (bed) in the lowest part of the ship, called steerage. In these dark, damp quarters well below the water line, the open space had been divided into tiny cabins. Bunk beds, two upper and two lower, had been roughed out of bare boards and fitted with straw-filled mattresses and pillows. Steerage passengers ate at rows of roughly made wooden tables in a central area.

Most passengers were seasick for the first week, many for the entire crossing. In the crowded quarters below deck the air was heavy with the smell of vomit, human sweat and the stomach-turning stench from the open buckets used as toilets.

Despite the miseries of the voyage, most traveled with high hopes. The lucky ones were met by family members who could help them through the first difficult months, providing a place to sleep and advice on how to find a job. But many found themselves stranded in a confusing world where few understood their language and some took advantage of them. Landlords charged high rents for dilapidated housing, and employers offered low wages while demanding more and more hours of work.

New immigrants often arrived with all their worldly goods in sacks on their backs.

WORKING WOMEN

Emily was used to the idea of women working. In her world, women always worked to help pay for their families' needs. Often women's jobs meant backbreaking labor — as servants in large houses, as washerwomen or as seamstresses. On the other hand, girls and women from well-to-do families were not allowed to work outside the home. From the day they left school until the day they married, these girls were expected to spend their time at home learning the art of housekeeping, so that they would know how to be good wives and mothers.

Emily didn't want to be like either of these groups. She aspired to be the kind of working woman Miss Henderson was — educated, decided in her opinions and independent. And by 1912 this was possible. Some jobs were seen as "respectable" and suitable for girls and women, at least for the few years before they married. Emily wanted one of those jobs so that she could leave poverty behind. But girls, from well-to-do families or not, still had only a few choices, and most of those choices depended on how much education they had.

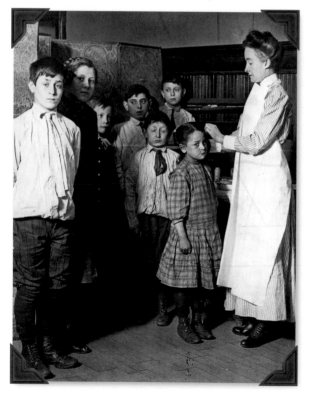

NURSE

Nursing had become a respectable career because of the crusading work of Florence Nightingale, a nurse who revolutionized the care of the wounded during the Crimean War of 1854 to 1856. By the 1890s many hospitals had schools of nursing. Competition to get into these schools was fierce, and those who were accepted had to have families willing and able to support them through the two-year course.

Some nurses brought much needed medical care to slum neighborhoods.

TEACHER

Girls who had stayed in school until they were sixteen might become teachers in a rural, one-room school for a few years. Many used their salaries to get more education so that they could apply for a position in a city school.

Teaching was a desirable occupation for an educated young woman.

MILLINER

A girl with nimble fingers and a flair for style might be apprenticed to train as a milliner, or hat maker. An apprentice was not paid until she had learned the craft, however, so this job was available only to girls whose families could afford to support them while they learned.

SALES CLERK

Small shops, often run by one family, were giving way to large department stores with many sales clerks. Since no training was needed, this became a popular job with many girls and young women. However, the long hours of standing and the poor pay made clerking only slightly better than factory jobs.

OFFICE WORKER

In their final year of school girls could learn such office skills as typing, shorthand and bookkeeping. Offices were now being staffed by "lady typists" instead of the male clerks of former years, so there were many positions available. But, as with factory work, employers offered women much smaller salaries than those of the men they had replaced.

(below) Large department stores employed many female clerks in their billing offices.

(right) Girls with neat handwriting could become office clerks.

TELEPHONE OPERATOR

The advent of the telephone created a need for switchboard operators who connected one telephone line with another to complete a call. The job required dexterity, a courteous manner and a pleasant speaking voice and so was ideal for teenaged girls and young women. But while these jobs were prized over factory work because of the clean working conditions, the wages were only slightly better. Long-distance operators also ran the risk of electrical shocks.

The expanded use of telephones opened new job opportunities for girls and women as telephone operators.

CHAPTER 4

The Interloper

Emily threw a finished shirtwaist onto the pile and reached for another. This place. Each day just like the last. Hour after boring hour. Minute after tedious minute. Too much time to think about the worries eating away at her.

"Check at the post office, Emmy," Mam had said yesterday morning, just as she'd said once every week for the past three months. What's the use? Emily wondered. Why don't we face the truth? But looking at her mother's strained, pale face, she had just muttered, "Yes, Mam." And, of course, when she raced to the post office on her short lunch break, she got nothing more than a shake of the postal clerk's head. Next week, she vowed, next week I will not …

"You! Get out of here."

The sudden shout made every head at the clipping table whip around. Dolly was leaning out the fire-escape door waving a threatening fist at someone on the stairs. What was going on? The noon bell rang and, like birds lifting off a pond, the clipping girls flocked around Dolly.

"One of those newspaper guys." Dolly banged the door shut. "I heard he's been hanging around the factories. Now you listen to me." She pointed at one girl after another. "No talking to him. Anything bad about us in the papers and Joe closes down the shop — just like that." Dolly snapped her fingers and the girls retreated, twittering anxiously. "Don't you forget, now."

"What do you mean — closes the shop?" Emily asked.

"Just what I said. Nosy reporters. Any trouble — anything gets into the papers — and we all lose our jobs. You. Me. Everybody. Joe don't want no trouble."

What kind of trouble? Emily wanted to ask, but Dolly was already striding off down the room. Would Magda know? Emily clattered down the metal stairs to where the clipping girls perched on the lowest steps. When she arrived their whispering stopped. Hunched over their open lunch pails they huddled together.

Emily turned to Magda, who shrugged. "They scared."

"But ..."

"Dolly say not talk. So — not." Magda settled in to chew stolidly through her crust of coarse brown bread.

Emily wanted to protest, but all she could do was yawn. I'm too tired. Too tired and too hungry to be bothered. She rested her head against the wall as she chewed her own chunk of bread. I could sleep for a year, she thought, and her eyelids drooped. Some days the littlest girls had to be shaken hard to wake them when the bell rang again.

After too few restful moments Emily forced her eyes open. Magda would want to read. And she was doing so well. Emily was astonished at how determined, desperate even, Magda was to learn. The other girls were interested, too. Some even watched over Magda's shoulder and mouthed the words with her. It was as if there was some magic about being able to read English.

What good do they think it will do? Look at me. Working in a factory just like them. Still, if Magda wants to ... She sat up and stretched. Through blurry, half-open eyes she saw a shape at the end of the alley.

"Is that the reporter? What long legs he has! Like a stork." Emily turned to share the joke, but Magda was on her feet.

"Shlekter!" she shouted. Two of the other girls leaped up beside her. All three surged forward, stamping their feet and making shooing motions as though the intruder were an unruly chicken. Their bulk filled the narrow alley, blocking Emily's view. On an impulse she ran up the steps to see over their heads. In the narrow strip of light at the mouth of the alley she could see him backing away, his hands spread placatingly. They must look fierce, she thought, as he jammed on his cap and ran.

What would a reporter want with factory girls? Emily puzzled over the mystery on the way home after work.

"Hey, wait up." The voice was deep and growly. Emily spun around. A tall, thin figure was loping toward her.

"You're the one who speaks English, aren't you? I heard you with those girls."

The interloper! "What do you want?"

"Just want to ask a couple of questions." Something about the way he smiled reminded Emily of Magda shouting, *"Shlekter!"* Bad one. And Dolly had warned them, too.

With a panicky flutter in her stomach Emily turned and started walking. "Go away."

"Listen, I'll level with you." He kept up with her easily, his long legs taking one step to two of hers. "My boss — all he wants is a little chat with someone who works in a factory, find out what it's like, how they treat you, that sort of thing."

She stopped and looked right at him. "Your boss? Who's that?"

"E.D. Harris of the *Globe*," he announced importantly.

"So you are a reporter." Then she saw that his cheeks were smooth and soft and showed no sign of a beard. "No. You're not old enough."

His cheeks reddened. "Office boy," he said defensively. "But I'm learning the business. And they'll make me a reporter as soon as I bring in a good story."

A good story? Was that what Dolly meant? Emily's heart beat harder. She quickened her pace and pushed ahead into the crush of pedestrians.

He caught up with her. "What harm can it do to talk?"

"A lot of harm. Go away!" Dodging pedestrians, looking straight ahead, she could still feel him close behind her.

A shout brought her up short.

"Em! Hey, Em!"

She turned sharply and caught her breath at the sight of Ernie hobbling toward her. Then she saw his face. "What happened to you?"

"Aw, one a' them big guys." He ran his tongue gingerly over his lower lip, swollen and oozing blood. "Said it was his corner. Shoulda run when Alfie did." He noticed the stranger hovering. "Who's this, then?"

"Carson. I'm Pete Carson. Listen, I'll see you around, okay?" And with a shrug, he loped off back the way they'd come.

Well, that got rid of him, anyway. "Oh, Ernie. Getting beaten up on the street. What's become of us?"

"It's nothin', Em. But listen. Great news! Before that bully came along, I sold ten papers. That's the most yet. And Alf'll find us another corner tomorrow."

But Ernie's cheerful tone couldn't hide from Emily his limp or the way he kept touching the rapidly darkening bruise under his eye.

He's just a little boy, she thought, as they trudged home together. He shouldn't have to sell papers so we can eat.

Next morning, on the way to work, Emily was still raging over the injustice of it all. It wasn't just the factory job or Ernie getting beaten up. Or spending the night helping Mam with a crying baby. When they'd arrived home yesterday they'd found Mam pacing up and down, a whimpering Annie in her arms.

"They said no," she'd burst out the minute Emily was in the door. "Not one cent, because we don't go to church. And they wouldn't even listen when I said Sunday was the only day we had for laundry. And now poor little Annie …" She buried her face in the baby's blanket to muffle her sobs. Emily had never seen her mother in such a state.

They'd felt so sure when they'd talked it over. A neighbor had told them how helpful the ladies at the church were. Mam would never have asked if she hadn't needed medicine for Annie's croup.

She was so deep in thought that Pete's voice coming out of the crowd startled her.

"Not you again. I can't —"

"Please," he interrupted, "let me explain. It's not just about a story for the papers. There're people who want to help. Influential people."

"I don't know what you're talking about."

"This is important. It's Em, right, what your brother called you?"

"No, it's Emily."

"If you'd listen just for a minute, Emily. What if I told you that people who can change things want to help."

"Help who? Help me? No one cares what happens to the likes of me!"

"Yes, you. And anybody else who works in a factory. Anybody who's treated badly by their bosses."

Like Sonia who lost all her pay? Like the clipping girls standing all day?

As though he'd read her thoughts, Pete said, "It's happened other places, you know. The mayor, well-to-do ladies, people like that — speaking out and getting factories cleaned up. Lots of people want to help." He paused and seemed to be making up his mind about something. Then, "Listen. I could introduce you to a lady — she lives uptown in one of those big houses. She knows powerful people in the government. She wants to change things. But we can't do it without proof. We have to know firsthand what's going on in there. And mostly we can't find out because no one speaks English. That's why you're so important."

"But Dolly says …" She caught herself and started again. "If anyone talks to the papers, the bosses will just close the factories. What will happen to us then?"

"Close the factories? How would they make money? They're just trying to scare you."

Emily thought about Joe, chewing his everlasting cigar, shouting at the clipping girls, shouting even at Dolly. Sneaking about on his rubber-soled shoes, threatening to fire anyone who talked or made even the tiniest mistake. There was no place in Joe's factory for Miss Henderson's dignity of the worker. But what if things *could* change?

As the thoughts raced through her head she'd been walking quickly. Now she slowed down. "Maybe …"

"Yes?"

She stopped suddenly. Right ahead of them was Magda's corner. "I can't. Go away." But it was too late. Magda had turned the corner and was staring right at them.

Emily turned fiercely on Pete. "Go away!" Then she hurried forward.

"You talk that *shlekter*?" Magda hissed through gritted teeth. She took a step forward and her hands were on Emily's shoulders, pushing her. "You lose us job!"

"Stop that!" Emily stumbled backward. Her head smacked against the brick wall and her lunch pail clattered to the sidewalk. "How dare you push me." She was about to shove back when she saw tears in Magda's angry eyes.

She dropped her hands. "Listen, Magda, he wants to help.

Clean up that filthy place. Get us fair pay. The newspaper could change things," she was surprised to hear herself say. "Make them better."

"Pfff!" Magda's hand flashed up in a scornful gesture, and Emily ducked. "He write in paper, how I buy bread? Little sisters starve in street!" Magda spat the last word so fiercely that Emily felt a spray of saliva. She put a trembling hand up to wipe her face.

"Now — you promise!" And with each word, Magda poked a hard finger at Emily's shoulder. "No — talk!" She stalked off, leaving Emily to trail after her, feeling defeated.

All morning, as Emily worked beside a still simmering Magda, the knot of misery in her stomach grew. Trouble at home and now Magda mad at her. And for what? Some stupid idea from a boy who wasn't even a real reporter? Magda was right. What could any of them do about the way things were here?

Filthy floors. Dust in the air so thick it made Katya cough until she spat up blood. And just yesterday there was Anna, fired when a sewing machine needle ran through her finger and blood stained the sleeve she was sewing. Her hysterical screams of "Please, no..." as she was bundled out the door still sounded in Emily's ears.

Why didn't Dolly stop Joe? She helped Magda. But Magda hadn't ruined a piece of fabric. Magda hadn't lost Joe money. No, Pete's wrong and Magda's right. No one can stop Joe — not the newspapers, not important people, not anyone. The boss does make the rules.

Well, Emily thought, gritting her teeth, if there's no way to change things for everybody, then I have to find a way to change things for me. The idea had come into her head that morning when she saw Anna's sewing machine sitting unused.

Now, as she worked, Emily mulled over the possibility. Seamstresses made two dollars more a week than clipping girls. With an extra two dollars Mam could take Annie to the doctor and paying the rent wouldn't be such a worry. She peeked again at the silent machine. How different could it be from Mam's? The one that had gone to the pawnshop to pay the rent in those desperate days just before they'd been thrown out onto the street.

A saying of Dad's popped into her head, "The Lord helps them as helps themselves." Do I dare? Her throat went dry at the thought of approaching Dolly. Think of Mam, she told herself. Mam and the little ones.

At the end of the day Emily dawdled. Magda didn't even look back as she and the other clipping girls headed for the door. Emily was standing alone by Anna's machine when Dolly came sailing past, arms piled high with finished shirts. "Out you go," Dolly said, not even looking at her.

"Wait! I need to ask you …" Dolly gave an impatient sigh, and Emily forgot all about the careful argument she'd worked out that afternoon. "I can run a sewing machine," she blurted out.

Dolly shook her head but, desperate, Emily plunged on. "Look — I made this blouse I'm wearing. What could it hurt to let me try? And then you wouldn't have to go looking for another seamstress."

She grasped the broken back of the sewing machine chair, staring earnestly at Dolly, trying to will away the skeptical look on her face.

"Joe don't like girls as young as you on the machines." Dolly cast an uneasy glance toward the front of the shop where Joe sat working on a pile of papers. "Oh well, let's see what you can do." She pulled a sleeve from a pile. "This machine does the seam, then passes on to the next for the cuff."

Emily drew a deep breath and sat down. Now that she had her chance, she felt surprisingly calm and confident. You can do this, she told herself. Mam was a good teacher. Very particular about neatness.

Emily slid the edge of the basted seam under the needle. Her hand went automatically to the wheel to lower the needle and anchor the sleeve. Pleased that her fingers remembered how to manipulate fabric and machine, she ran the seam quickly, cut the thread, then held out the sleeve for inspection.

"Not bad." Dolly sounded surprised. "Not bad at all. Okay, we'll give you a trial run. See what you can do. Oh, and by the way, the cost of the thread comes out of your pay packet, so don't waste any."

Dolly turned away, and Emily let her breath out in a long sigh of relief. Even paying for her own thread, she'd be taking home more money than before. And she could sit all day! So what if the chair had a broken back. Then, with a pang, Emily remembered the frail woman who'd worked this machine. Where would Anna get another job? How would she feed her children and pay the rent?

She pushed away the prickle of guilt. Somebody will get this job, she reminded herself. Joe won't let a machine sit idle for long. She remembered Dad saying, "It's an ill wind that blows no one good." Now I know what that means — Anna's bad luck is my good luck.

BOYS AT WORK

Emily worried about her brother Ernie. In their old neighborhood friendly (and nosy) neighbors kept a close watch on the children. Any mischief was quickly reported to the parents. But in this new, poorer neighborhood, Ernie could get into all sorts of trouble. At age ten, he still went to school. But there were lots of free hours after school and on the weekends.

Once Ernie completed his job of picking up and delivering the sewing that his mother did at home, he was free to wander. When Alfie offered to show him how the neighborhood boys spent their spare hours, Ernie was delighted. Alfie's most useful lesson was about scavenging.

SCAVENGING

Many boys were expected to help out with the family finances by finding coal to fuel the cooking stove and scavenging saleable items from the garbage dump (or elsewhere).

Boys cobbled together small, wheeled carts to help in their scavenging expeditions.

Scavenging for coal required resourcefulness. One way was to walk along the train tracks picking up lumps that had fallen from the coal cars of the steam trains that roared through the city. Fire trucks were also coal-burning. So another way the boys got coal was to run after the fire trucks shouting rude insults until the exasperated firemen pelted them with lumps of coal. But finding coal was no laughing matter. Without coal to take home a boy had to scavenge behind stores for wood from broken crates or anything else that would burn.

Boys carrying burlap sacks flocked like sparrows to the city's garbage dump. They searched for rags and glass bottles to sell for a few pennies to a rag and bone man. Every so often a boy might strike it lucky and come across such treasures as an unbroken teapot or a stool with all its legs. These items could be sold at the local pawnshop, earning far more than rags and bottles.

NEWSIES

Boys with a few coins in their pockets could go into business for themselves. One of the easiest ways was by selling newspapers. After school each day boys flocked to the office of the local newspaper to buy as many newspapers as they could afford. Then they spread out along the downtown streets anxious to sell every paper. Unsold ones could not be returned and were wasted money.

The bigger, tougher boys staked out the best territory — busy corners, street-car stops or the entranceways to large office buildings — and defended it with their fists. Younger boys like Ernie and Alfie ran up and down the streets waving newspapers at pedestrians or tried sneaking onto the back of a streetcar to sell a few papers before the conductor threw them off. With luck and hard work a boy might work his way up to two dozen papers a day. Then he could save up enough money to set himself up as a shoeshine boy.

A newsie sells his papers.

SHOESHINE BOYS

By shining shoes a boy could make five to seven dollars a week in a busy downtown area. A shine cost ten cents, and men willing to pay for a shine were often also good tippers. Boys who couldn't afford their own shoeshine kit (a box, rags and polish) worked for men who provided them with the equipment — and who also took most of the profits.

MESSENGER BOYS

Boys on bicycles zoomed all over the downtowns of cities, delivering messages or goods. Some boys delivered telegrams. The telegraph companies wanted their messengers to look smart, so they issued uniforms with peaked caps. Fifty cents a week was kept back from the boys' wages for these uniforms, a real hardship when the boys earned only a few dollars a week. Even so, many boys left school at thirteen to become full-time messenger boys.

Men often stopped for a shoeshine on their way to work.

For a few years they earned a living that helped their families survive. Then, at sixteen, they found themselves replaced by younger boys. Now they were not only unemployed but also lacked the education or training to get another kind of job.

Smart uniforms set messenger boys apart from other boys on the streets.

SOMEBODY, PLEASE HELP!

Factory owners knew that workers desperately needed jobs. They also knew that they could easily replace workers who quit or were fired. So they felt no pressure to spend money on improvements to make the factories clean and safe. As dirt and disease from the slums and factory areas began to affect the rest of the city, a number of groups realized that something had to be done. The most public voice was that of the newspapers.

Some newspapers felt it was their responsibility to stop abuses in factories and improve conditions in slums. Investigative reporters were sent out to find the story behind the story: who was to blame, why weren't they stopped, what should be done?

Headlines show the growing desperation of the poor.

One scandal that attracted the attention of many newspapers across North America was the treatment of child workers. To get the inside story, reporters like Pete tried to talk to workers on their way to and from work. Were the workers underage? Underpaid? Angry? Ready to talk about it?

Newspapers needed exciting stories to sell papers, but many were also sincere in their desire to help improve the lives of the poor. And because almost everyone read newspapers, the owners knew they had a powerful voice. The factory owners knew that, too. They didn't want anyone exposing what went on behind factory doors. Threatening to fire anyone who talked to newspaper reporters was one way the factory owners fought back.

THE FIGHT TO IMPROVE SOCIAL CONDITIONS

In the early 1900s governments did almost nothing to help the poor. The attitude of the day was: If you're poor it's your own fault — work harder and you'll succeed. But some people realized that simply working harder wasn't always the answer. What about people hurt in accidents caused by dangerous factory equipment? What about young mothers with babies? What about children? The plight of the poor troubled a number of organizations. Gradually churches, Benevolent Societies and Settlement Houses mobilized to help those who were having difficulty helping themselves.

The squalor and crowded conditions in many boarding houses angered social reformers.

BENEVOLENT SOCIETIES

In some European cities workers had set up insurance funds to help those who fell on hard times. When immigrants arrived in the New World they were keen to continue this self-help program, so they set up Benevolent Societies. These societies were organized by country of origin. Members of the Italian Benevolent Society, for example, would meet incoming immigrant ships or trains, looking for Italian-speaking immigrants. They offered help in finding homes and jobs, often settling the newcomers in an area close to others who spoke their language.

Once they had jobs, immigrants paid the society a few pennies a week. If a family member couldn't work because of sickness or an accident, the family could ask for a small amount of money to pay the rent or buy food. Because they had paid their dues in good times, they felt no shame in asking for help in bad times.

CHURCHES

Some people could not afford even the small sum necessary to belong to a Benevolent Society. They turned to the churches, which provided soup kitchens, used clothing and bedding and kept small funds of money to hand out to those in desperate need. Churches worked hard to help the poor, but many of the needy felt shy about approaching a church they didn't belong to or where no one spoke their language. They needed a place that was welcoming to all. That place was the local Settlement House.

SETTLEMENT HOUSES

By the early 1900s big cities had organizations right in the heart of slum neighborhoods dedicated to helping the working poor no matter where they came from. These Settlement Houses were started by social workers and paid for by wealthy reformers. Settlement Houses provided classes in English, sewing, cooking and baby care. They also provided meeting rooms so neighbors could get to know one another as they chatted or relaxed over a favorite game.

In slum areas, where dirt and lack of sanitation led to such diseases as tuberculosis and typhoid fever, Settlement Houses also provided much-needed health care. Nurses or doctors paid for by the Settlement House ran clinics for the sick. Once a month a "well-baby" clinic would help mothers who often knew very little about how to keep their children healthy.

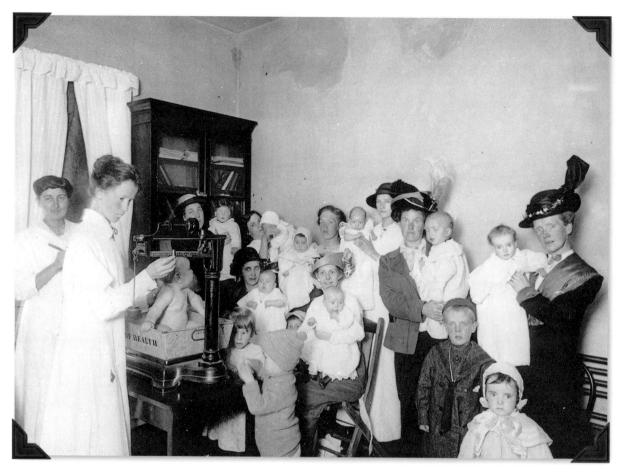

The local Settlement House often made the difference between a family's success or failure. The idea started with two women: Jane Addams and Ellen Gates Starr.

Settlement Houses ran "well-baby" clinics for poor families.

JANE ADDAMS AND ELLEN GATES STARR

One day in 1889 the residents of a slum in Chicago were surprised to find that a decaying brick house in their midst had new tenants. The two young women who had moved in were much too well dressed to belong to the working poor. So what were they doing here?

As the young women, Jane Addams and Ellen Gates Starr, cleaned and painted and refurbished the old mansion, the

Jane Addams

Ellen Gates Starr

neighbors watched warily. Then one day Jane and Ellen invited some of the children into the kitchen for milk and spaghetti. What could this mean? Gradually, over days and weeks, suspicion and mistrust faded. First the children, then the women, then the men appeared at the door. Whether it was for a bowl of soup at the end of a working day or a comfortable chat over tea and biscuits, the residents of one of Chicago's bleakest slums had found a haven at Hull House.

Hull House offered a day care for children of working mothers, classes in English, cooking and sewing and a club room for meetings. To encourage women to take pride in their origins, Jane invited them to display the crafts from their home countries. She also arranged for speakers to help educate them in the ways of the New World.

Jane and Ellen often charged small fees for these services so their visitors wouldn't feel they were taking charity, but the pennies and nickels they collected came nowhere near to paying the running costs of Hull House. For that, Jane needed donations from her parents' wealthy friends. She was such a persuasive speaker that she soon had many people interested in helping Hull House. And as she had hoped, her idea spread. Other reformers raised money to open Settlement Houses in their own communities. Soon the slum neighborhoods of every industrial city in North America had at least one.

Settlement Houses showed that a little bit of help could vastly improve the lives of the working poor. But they also showed that much more could be done. Reformers soon realized that private donations weren't enough. They needed to convince governments to pass laws that would provide services for the working poor and the unemployed — the "down and out" of society.

THE REFORMERS

Women like Jane Addams and Ellen Gates Starr lived in the slums and tried to improve the lives of the poor on a day-to-day basis. But the problems were so large and so widespread that other reformers realized government intervention was necessary. Laws needed to be changed.

Many reformers were well-to-do women who formed such groups as the National

In filthy surroundings, many children were constantly sick.

Council of Women of Canada. They approached politicians they knew socially and attempted to persuade them to use their power to improve the lives of poor workers, particularly of children and women.

Why would women who had easy lives themselves spend so much time working on behalf of the poor? Most were strongly religious and felt compelled to help those less fortunate. But they also knew that by improving the lives of the poor they were also protecting their own families. The filthy, rat-infested slums bred diseases such as smallpox, typhoid fever and cholera, which could spread quickly into the wealthier areas of the city. Laws that forced cities to provide clean drinking water, install sewage systems and clean up garbage that attracted vermin protected not only the poor but all the city's children.

THE PAWNSHOP

Emily, Ernie and Mrs. Watson had discussed endlessly over their soup suppers the question that scared them all. What if, one day, they couldn't afford to pay the rent? They all agreed, there was only one thing they could do.

And so the day that Mam's purse held not one penny, Ernie ran to get his little wooden pushcart, and

Pawnshops offered an essential service to slum residents.

Emily hefted her mother's sewing machine into it. It was their most valuable possession, the only thing they could take to the pawnshop that would bring enough money to pay the rent they owed.

Children carrying goods to the local pawnshop were a common sight in poor neighborhoods where families often found themselves without enough money to pay the rent or buy food. The lucky ones had some valuable article that the pawnbroker would take in return for a small amount of money. It might be grandpa's pocket watch, a wedding ring or a prized china teapot. For some, the only article that would bring in money was something as necessary as a winter coat. When payday came one of the children was sent to the pawnshop to redeem the pawned item.

The pawnbroker promised to keep the article for one month. If the owner was able to pay back the loan along with an extra charge called interest, he could get his goods back. All too often, at the end of the month, workers had no money to reclaim their possessions. Instead they were so short of money that they had to pawn something else. In bad times families could lose all their possessions, one by one, to the pawnbroker, with no hope of ever buying them back.

93

CHAPTER 5

The Visitor

"I'm sure I had it. It must be in my pocket." Emily scrambled up from the floor where she'd been on her knees frantically feeling around the treadle of her machine. For the third time, she plunged her hand into her pocket. Nothing. But where was it? She'd been so careful. She'd watched the other seamstresses and, just like them, every evening she'd tucked her spool of thread into her apron pocket for safekeeping, then rolled the apron up to carry it home. But this morning, when she'd unrolled her apron, the spool was missing. She felt tears start and gave a big sniff to stop them.

"Okay, kid. Okay." Dolly reached into her apron pocket and handed Emily another spool. "Just get on with your stint."

Behind her Emily heard Joe snarl, "What did I tell you? She's too blasted young."

"Joe, Joe …" Dolly's voice took on the placating tone she always used with the boss. "Lots of spools get lost. I'll mark it down. It comes off her pay."

Emily felt a pang. Fifty cents off. The first time she'd been docked for anything. Ten whole loaves of bread that fifty cents would have bought them. With shaking hands she fitted the spool onto the machine's spindle. And now she was behind with her work as well. That was the other unexpected thing about this job — what Dolly called her "stint." She had to sew up at least sixty seams an hour or stay behind until she'd finished. In the two weeks she'd been at this machine she'd always managed. Until today.

Halfway through the morning Joe came striding back. He stopped right behind Emily, and her heart jumped. Had he seen her wipe the sweat off her forehead with the back of her hand? Was he going to yell at her for getting grubby finger marks on the clean, white material? But Joe's bark, when it came, was directed at the clipping table girls.

"You. You. And you." He pointed at the three smallest girls, the cigar glowing between his fingers. "Into the box. Now!"

Dolly arrived. Shifting her load of shirts to one arm, she leaned over to brush the ash off the table. Only the set of her mouth showed what she thought of Joe and his cigar.

"Quickly, now. In with you." She herded the three girls in front of her. In the corner was a tall wooden crate that had once held bolts of fabric. Dolly dragged a chair in front of it, and Emily watched in amazement as each girl climbed onto the chair and clambered into the box.

"Scrunch down," Dolly ordered and, as soon as all three heads had disappeared, she dumped her pile of shirts in on top.

"The rest of you, stand tall and look busy, if you know what's good for you," Joe growled as he headed toward the front of the shop. "Dolly! Clear that aisle."

Dolly gestured to Magda and the two of them shoved bales of fabric back against the wall away from the door to the back stairs.

Waves of dust rose from the floor. Emily's nose twitched and the woman beside her sneezed. Filthy place, Emily thought. They could at least sweep up the fluff and clippings. Then, as Magda passed her, she leaned over and whispered, "What's happening?" Magda had been stiff and distant for days after the incident with Pete, but this morning she had waited at the corner for Emily.

Magda put her finger to her lips. "Inspector," she mouthed and turned away.

Inspector? Good! Maybe he'll do something about the dirt. But … maybe not. Magda had explained to her one day about the inspector.

"He come every three, four month. Stay few minutes. He no see little girls, he no care anything." She'd shrugged and, with a cynical twist to her mouth, added, "Joe pay him."

Well, I'm not going to be taken for underage, Emily vowed, tucking a few stray hairs behind her ear and patting the bun at the back of her neck. Twisting her long hair into a knot had made her feel so grown-up the first day she'd come to the factory. Now it was going to help her keep this job. That extra two dollars had already smoothed some of the lines from Mam's forehead.

With a click the main shop door opened. All along the line of sewing machines heads turned.

A couple came into the factory — a man and a woman. Emily heard a shocked intake of breath from the seamstress next to her. A woman inspector! Hadn't Magda said it was always just one man? That he walked around quickly, then left? And this woman … Even from halfway down the room, Emily was struck by her elegant outfit. She knew if she could run her fingers over the deep plum of the long skirt, it would be as soft as a cloud. And such a hat! This was not just any woman, this was a lady — and judging by the way she was inspecting her surroundings, a formidable one.

Joe seemed to be objecting, his head bobbing vigorously as he sawed the air with his arms. He looked angry, but Emily couldn't make out any words over the din of the machines. She reached for a new sleeve and spotted Dolly standing to one end of the clipping table, arms loaded with shirtwaists. Her face was rigid and watchful. Something's up, Emily thought. This definitely isn't a usual inspection.

Emily turned back to her work, but her ears told her what a flutter of interest the visitor had caused. Instead of a steady din from the sewing machines, the sound dipped up and down as heads turned for surreptitious glances.

"Nevertheless, Mr. Kerenski …" A clear, high voice cut into one of the lulls. "Nevertheless, I say, the mayor himself has asked my committee for a report. So I will look for myself." The lady visitor turned an appraising glance on the room. "It seems very dark in here. I wonder how these women can see to work."

It was the voice of someone used to getting her own way. Emily suddenly realized who she must be — one of the ladies Pete had talked about. One of the do-gooders who wanted to clean up the factories. And what was that about the mayor? She turned to have a better look and found her glance caught by the visitor's sharp eyes. They seemed to bore right into her. Emily turned away quickly, afraid her face might give away just how young she really was.

Emily had her eyes locked on her work, her fingers guiding a sleeve under her clattering needle, when she felt the swish of a skirt passing. What was the visitor up to now? Out of the corner of one eye Emily could see the lady leaning over

Magda. "Now tell me, dear …" Her voice was encouraging. "How old are you?"

Magda shrugged and turned away with an abrupt, "No speak English."

From the wooden crate in the corner came a muffled thud. The visitor's head swiveled, the feather on her broad-brimmed hat quivering.

Dolly was beside the box in a flash. "Sorry," she said. "Tripped." And she calmly dumped her armload of shirts onto the ones already in the crate.

The lady turned, and Emily, bent over her work, felt the skirt swish behind her again, heard the tapping of leather heels. Good. She was gone. The danger was past.

"What's this?" The tapping heels stopped, then returned. She was right behind Emily. "Your chair back is broken."

Does she mean me? Emily stopped her machine, her heart pounding. What if she asks my age? I'll have to lie. "It's … it's all right, thank you, ma'am. I don't need … I always sit forward to work."

"Ah! You speak English."

Emily's heart lurched. "Yes, ma'am," she muttered, her head bent over her work.

"Then tell me, my dear, why are there so few workers at the clipping table? Are these young women away sick? Or are they, perhaps, elsewhere on the premises?"

What if I point to the girls in the crate? What if I tell about money taken from pay packets? Will Joe have to explain to the mayor? Will he have to treat us better? Emily took a deep breath, half-turned on her chair and found herself looking straight into Magda's eyes. And as the words formed on her lips she saw the squalid room, the four little sisters with no dinner. She heard Magda's plea, Who buy bread if I no work?

"I — I ..." Emily stuttered and stopped.

"Yes, my dear?"

"I couldn't say, ma'am."

"Well, what about underage girls — are there any employed here?"

"I don't know about that either, ma'am." Out of the corner of her eye Emily could see Joe sidling down the aisle. "You'll have to ask Mr. Kerenski."

"Very well, my dear. I believe I understand."

Emily's heart gave another lurch. Understand what? And then Joe was at her elbow, glaring. She straightened the sleeve under the needle and was about to press on the foot treadle when the lady's voice rang out again.

"Young woman!"

Emily jumped, but the lady visitor had sailed past her and was pointing a gloved finger at Dolly. "I wish to see the ladies' retiring room."

Joe gave an abrupt nod. Dolly whirled and headed for the back corridor, the lady right behind her.

"Back to work, the lot of you," Joe hissed as he stalked along the aisle to his desk at the front of the shop.

Cautiously Emily watched his progress. She saw him exchange glances with the inspector, who was leaning against the wall, arms folded. The man shrugged as if to say, Nothing I can do about it. Scowling, Joe sat down and began shuffling through a stack of papers.

Emily had finished several more sleeves by the time the sharp voice again cut through the din of the sewing machines.

"Mr. Kerenski, I am appalled. Appalled, sir. The working conditions for these women are unsafe, unsanitary and degrading. This factory floor is filthy. There are highly flammable scraps scattered about. And as for the retiring room. Well! However, I have found no direct infraction of the current laws. I assure you, nevertheless, that my committee intends to do something to improve these conditions."

Joe was on his feet now, his hands waving as though to dismiss her charges. But the lady was not finished.

"You may rest assured, Mr. Kerenski, we will find a way to force changes. And *that* I promise you."

As the door clicked behind the pair Emily could almost feel the whole shop relax. They still had jobs. No one was going to shut them down — yet. But Joe wasn't happy. For the rest of the morning he prowled the shop, growling at this one, snarling at that one. He stood glaring at the three smallest girls who had clambered out of the crate as soon as the visitors left. Finally one of them, hands shaking, clipped too close to the fabric and Joe pounced.

"Two cents off!" He threw his cigar down and ground it into the floor with his heel.

The sound of the lunchtime bell was a relief to everyone. As though the visit had somehow made them allies again, Magda sat beside Emily on the fire-escape stairs. She bit into her bread, chewed slowly, swallowed, then asked, "Why you no tell?"

"What do you mean?"

"You talk that guy. Why no tell lady?"

How could she explain? She hardly knew herself. Was it Magda's plea? Or knowing how desperately Mam needed her pay packet? Perhaps it was just plain cowardice. Finally all she could do was shrug.

But Magda's question kept niggling at her. All afternoon, as she sewed one seam after another, she tried to sort it out. Should I have spoken out? No matter what the cost? Too late now. But next time …?

The clang of the finishing bell startled her out of her absorption. Ten seams left to finish, she realized with annoyance. It was the first time she hadn't finished her stint since she started. As Magda and the other girls trooped out, she sat on, her machine chattering. And she wasn't the only one. The morning's interruption had slowed down a number of the seamstresses, who were hurrying to complete their stints.

By the time she'd dragged herself home she was starving. Would there be any of yesterday's bread and cheese left? She had just pushed open the door when a burst of laughter stopped her. Three happy faces turned toward her.

"Emily! Here you are at last!" Mam was sitting at the table as usual, sewing buttons onto one of the factory coats. And there, sitting across from her with his long legs tucked under their table, looking perfectly at home, was the young reporter.

What was going on?

"You must hear Pete's story about the time he was chased by the organ-grinder's monkey," Mam said, as Pete politely jumped to his feet to offer her his chair.

"What are you doing here?"

"I brought him," Ernie piped up. "He's a great guy, Em. He showed me 'n' Alf a terrific spot to sell papers — right where people get off the streetcars. They're in such a hurry half of 'em don't even wait for change. Me 'n' Alf sold every paper.

Look at that!" Ernie scooped a handful of coins off the table and let them cascade back down onto the wooden surface.

But Emily just tightened her lips and turned accusing eyes on the young reporter. "Why have you come?"

"I had some news to tell you about a public meeting. The speaker is a young woman all the way from New York City — Clara Lemlich. She used to be a garment worker. Look. I brought a handbill."

Emily waved it away. How dare he come bursting in here with his wild ideas? "Did you tell my mother what you really want? A good story so they'll make you a reporter? No matter what harm it does to the women who need those jobs?"

A blush started at his shirt collar and flamed all the way up to the roots of his hair.

"Yes," he said slowly, turning to a frowning Mam, "it's true. I do want to be a reporter. But I'm not just after a good story. Newspapers can help. They can make people think about how unfairly factory workers are treated. But nothing will change unless someone speaks up. Like Clara … Or …" He turned back to Emily with a look that made her cheeks go hot.

He couldn't know, she thought, that she'd had a chance that very day. Even so, his look left her too flustered to say anything.

"Well, anyway," Pete continued, "I'll just leave you this handbill. It's not for another week. You can think about whether … If you want to go, I'll be around." He backed toward the door, cap in hand. "Nice to meet you, Mrs. Watson."

As the door clicked behind him, Ernie said, "Aw, Em. We were havin' a real good time. Why'd you have to spoil it?"

"Leave Emily alone. She's tired. Come and have some

supper, Emmy." Mam's voice was warm and comforting.

Gratefully Emily sat down to bread and cheese. Hot tea soothed her insides and, slowly, the tightness in her forehead eased. Even the sharp clink of coins dropping into a bowl, as Ernie counted and recounted his newspaper earnings, ceased to feel like blows to her tired brain.

Her eyes strayed to the handbill that lay beside her on the table. Clara Lemlich glared back at her with fiery eyes. What a tiger she looks, Emily thought. If she'd been there this afternoon … Why, I'll bet she would have dragged that lady visitor right over to the box hiding those little girls.

Under the picture the handbill proclaimed, "Strike organizer! Tireless advocate of the power of unions! Undeterred by the catcalls of a hostile crowd or the fists of thugs." The fists of thugs! Emily shivered. Is that what speaking out got you? And yet it said — "undeterred."

Mam put down her sewing and rubbed her reddened eyes. "I've been thinking, Emmy, maybe this young woman has something useful to say. It wouldn't hurt just to listen to her. If it weren't for the babies, I might go, too."

Emily was speechless. Mam? At a protest rally?

Mam lifted her chin. "Someone has to do something." Then she gave a sigh. "But right now, I have to finish sewing on these buttons."

Emily picked up the handbill again and glanced at the words marching boldly across the bottom: "August 30th at 7:30 P.M. Labor Day Rally."

Labor Day. A week away. And the day after that Continuation School started. So that's that, then. She opened her fingers and the handbill fluttered to the floor.

THE HAZARDS OF FACTORY WORK

Emily was at her sewing machine, carefully guiding fabric under the needle. A sharp gasp from across the aisle made her start. Lifting her foot to stop her machine, she glanced up. The face across from her was contorted with pain. The woman seemed to be hiding one hand under the table. And there on the sleeve she had been sewing were two large splotches of blood. Emily shuddered.

Accidents happened often to workers exhausted from lack of sleep and poor diets. Minor cuts, abrasions and burns were common. A moment's hesitation near whirling or pounding machine parts could also mean fingers cut off or hair torn out by the roots.

Noise and pollution were also health hazards. The machines were sometimes so loud that workers had to shout to be heard. Particles of dust or chemicals in the air made them cough and wheeze. Everyone left at the end of the long workday with aching heads and wheezing chests. Years of working under these conditions could do permanent damage to eyes, lungs and hearing.

This boy's fingers are at risk as he removes a board from a cutting machine.

Other aspects of factory life were more unpleasant than dangerous. Owners often crowded as much equipment as possible into small spaces and provided few toilets and wash basins. In such crowded and unsanitary conditions disease spread quickly. Working in close quarters, lacking sleep and eating poorly, factory workers were at risk of developing the scourge of the poor: tuberculosis, a disease affecting the lungs.

The scariest hazard was the ever-present threat of fire. In garment factories one smoldering cigarette could turn fabric clippings piled in corners, under tables and in boxes into fire bombs. Escaping the fire was often difficult. Many factory buildings were old, with narrow staircases and unsafe fire escapes.

Cities passed laws to stop health and safety abuses. But the laws could be enforced only if city inspectors kept constant watch. Most cities had few inspectors, and too many of those were willing to take bribes to overlook dangerous conditions.

(left) Machinery with moving parts was dangerous in crowded factories.

THE POWER OF PICTURES

Many people who enjoyed the price and convenience of factory-made clothes preferred not to know about the working conditions of the people who made these inexpensive goods. They shrugged their shoulders, saying it was not their problem. The reformers wanted to change this attitude. But how could the plight of workers, especially working children, be made obvious so that neither the lawmakers nor the general public could refuse to face the facts? The answer: show them pictures.

In 1912 photographic equipment was still heavy and awkward. The camera was a large wooden box perched on a tripod. Although paper film was available, photographers preferred glass plates coated with chemicals. Despite the cumbersome equipment, photography had long since moved out of the studio. If war correspondents and explorers could show the realities of faraway places in pictures, reformers reasoned, then photographers closer to home could show the horrors of factories and slums.

Three dedicated reformers published their disturbing pictures in books and newspapers. The impact of these photographs started to slowly change public opinion.

JACOB RIIS

Jacob Riis, a police reporter for the *New York Tribune* newspaper, began photographing life in the slums of New York as early as the 1880s. He walked the slum streets at night, determined to get the "inside story." What he saw appalled him. In the attic of one tenement house he found a "man, his wife and three small children shivering in one room, through the roof of which the pitiless winds of winter whistled. The room was almost barren of furniture; the parents slept on the floor, the elder children in boxes and the baby was swung in an old shawl attached to the rafters by cords."

Jacob Riis

To show his readers how dire the conditions were, Riis took his camera and one of the first flash attachments into the slums "so that the darkest corner might be photographed." Then he organized his collection of photographs into a series of illustrated lectures aimed

106

Riis's pictures of sleeping children huddled outdoors made the public aware of the appalling conditions in city slums.

directly at people who had the money and power to change these appalling conditions. Using an early projector called a magic lantern, he cast his images of poverty onto a large screen. The dramatic pictures linked to his impassioned message moved audiences to tears. Story and images were spread even farther afield in his book *How the Other Half Lives*.

One influential person affected by Riis's horrific story was Theodore Roosevelt, Commissioner of Police for New York City in the 1890s and later President of the United States. By influencing powerful people like Roosevelt, Riis was able to help reformers working to improve housing, education and child labor laws.

Jacob Riis was born in Denmark in 1849. As a young man of twenty-one he immigrated to America. He understood how difficult it was to begin life in a new country. By the time he died in 1914 his ten books and stark pictures of the dark side of immigrant life had convinced many in America that something had to be done.

Lewis Hine

LEWIS HINE

Lewis Hine was a shy, quiet schoolteacher in New York City in 1904 when he attracted the attention of reformers interested in child welfare. They asked him to record the plight of child workers. Carrying his heavy box camera, Lewis Hine climbed dark staircases to visit sweatshops, talked his way into factories and canneries and crept into mine tunnels to capture previously untold stories.

Employers did not welcome him. None wanted the outside world to know about the underage workers who toiled for long hours in dangerous, unsanitary conditions. To get his pictures Hine often resorted to subterfuge. Claiming to be photographing the machinery, he would place a child worker in front merely, he said, to show the relative size of the machinery. If he was not allowed into a factory or mine, Hine waited at the gates until closing time. The ragged clothes, dirty faces and exhausted expressions of the children huddled in front of his camera told their own story of hardship and abuse.

For nearly ten years Hine traveled from one side of the United States to the other photographing children at work. Everywhere he went he asked questions: how old, how many hours a day, how much money a week, how long have you been here? When the photographs and information appeared in newspapers and magazines, they caused horror and outrage. No one who saw the careworn faces and stunted bodies of these young children could deny their suffering.

Hine went on to photograph soldiers at war in Europe from 1914 to 1918. But his greatest work was documenting the lives of exploited child workers.

A Hine photo of a child laborer

108

J.S. WOODSWORTH

John Shaver Woodsworth, a Methodist minister, saw firsthand the desperate lives of immigrants from Europe when he opened the All People's Mission in the north end of Winnipeg. Poles, Jews, Galicians and Germans came to the mission to learn English, bring their children to kindergarten, learn housekeeping skills or, in bad times, get food and clothing. Woodsworth saw that prejudice and ignorance made their lives even more difficult. How could he persuade people to accept these newcomers?

J.S. Woodsworth

One solution was to fight prejudice with knowledge. Woodsworth traveled across Canada and the United States preaching about the "Sin of Indifference." Using a magic lantern to enlarge photographs on the walls of churches and community halls, he challenged those more fortunate to look beyond the unfamiliar clothing and languages — to focus on the similarities rather than the differences.

In a book called *Strangers Within Our Gates,* Woodsworth implored churches everywhere to take on the work of helping the newcomers. But he soon realized that this piecemeal effort was not enough. By 1911, in *My Neighbour,* he was exhorting city councillors to clean up the slums. The next step, he realized, was to convince the federal government to pass countrywide laws to protect child and adult workers. In an attempt to make this happen, J.S. Woodsworth himself ran as a candidate for the 1921 federal election — and won. For the rest of his life he was involved in the fight for reform at the federal level.

Despite their dedication, Riis, Hine, Woodsworth and other reformers faced frustration after frustration. By 1916 the public in both Canada and the United States was demanding an end to the abuses of child labor. Governments tried to respond, but time after time, laws were proposed only to be struck down by courts that called them unconstitutional. Not until the Great Depression of the 1930s were strong laws passed to prevent the exploitation of underage workers. Sadly, this legislation was finally put in place because men needed the jobs that had previously been done more cheaply by children and teenagers.

Immigrant children attend a kindergarten class at the All People's Mission in Winnipeg.

Churches used posters to try to change negative attitudes toward immigrants.

CHAPTER 6

The Letter

With her hand on the doorknob, Emily hesitated. In her pocket she could feel the stiff outlines of the letter. That noon, when the postal clerk had handed her a letter with a Calgary postmark, her heart had nearly stopped. At last! Then she saw the unfamiliar handwriting. And no return address. What could it mean?

Suddenly the door opened and Mam was standing in the doorway, baby Annie on her hip. "I thought I heard you." Her forehead furrowed as she looked at Emily. "What is it?"

"There's a letter," Emily blurted out and saw hope spring into her mother's eyes.

"Oh, Emmy." Mam's free hand went to her heart. She backed into the small, dark room. "Quick, let me have it."

"Mam, it's not from Dad." But her mother had already snatched the letter.

"Here, take Annie." She thrust the baby at Emily.

Emily took the sleepy baby and laid her in the cradle, her mind on the letter. The afternoon had been almost unbearable — sitting and sewing for hours without knowing what was in it. But now, did she even want to know?

Mam was sitting at the table, studying the unfamiliar writing. "I'm afraid to open it." Her voice caught on the words and she swallowed. Then, with a shaking hand, she tore the flap and pulled out the folded paper. Something else fluttered out of the envelope and landed on her lap.

Dollar bills! Ten of them! Oh, thank goodness. It must be from Dad!

"Dear Mrs. Watson," Mam was reading out loud. "I am sorry to be the bearer of bad news …" Mam's voice faltered, her eyes skimming down the page. "Oh, Emmy. Oh, dear God, no."

Emily's heart gave a great thud. "What, Mam? What?"

"Your father … a mining accident." Emily could barely hear the hoarse whisper. "Not coming back … Dead." The letter dropped from her mother's hands.

Emily reached to pick it up. That can't be true. It mustn't be.

Desperately she scanned the pages. At the end was a scrawled signature — Liam O'Ryan, the workmate he'd traveled west with. She started at the top and made herself read every word. At first they'd found work with a builder. Yes, Dad's letters had told them that. He'd been so happy sending them money. After a few months, they were laid off. "But don't worry," Dad's last letter had said, "there's sure to be other work." No luck at the lumber camps, Liam's letter continued. And no money to pay their way home. So they decided to split up and Dad headed south to the silver mines in Montana.

The accident had happened soon afterward. Months later Liam finally tracked him down. Collected the pay Dad was owed. Had a marker put on his grave. "Dreadfully sorry for your loss."

Emily could barely take in the details. She looked up to see Mam staring vacantly into space. Feeling like a sleepwalker, Emily rose and walked around the table. She put her arms around her mother and, silently, they rocked back and forth.

That night as she lay beside Mam in the bed they shared, Emily felt despair settle like a stone on her chest. Eventually they had cried, exhausted themselves with their grief at losing Dad. But now all she could think of was tomorrow. How far would ten dollars take them? For a little while they didn't have to dread the weekly visit of the rent collector, but after that?

As tears slid down her cheeks she felt the bed heave. Mam, muffling a sob in her pillow. Was that for Dad? Or was she, too, thinking, There's no way out. We're trapped.

The next morning the effort of pushing herself out the door to go back to the factory was almost more than Emily could manage. But now, more than ever, she must earn that pay packet. Her head ached from all the tossing and turning of the night before, and she didn't notice Magda until she was almost beside her. With a guilty start she realized she had brought nothing for Magda to read. Well … too bad. She felt her face settle into tight, mean lines. What good would reading do her, anyway? Stuck in that dreadful factory.

Magda stopped in front of Emily and clasped her hands tightly together. Slowly and carefully she pronounced, "I-am-happy-to-see-you-this-morning." Then she ducked her head shyly. "Was good English, no?"

Emily forced herself to smile. "Very good," she said, in the same encouraging tone Miss Henderson had always used. She was about to say "I'm sorry we can't read today …" when Magda reached into her pocket.

"For you I have sometink …" It still came out "tink" even though Emily had been emphasizing pronunciation in their reading lessons. Magda held out a tight square of material, then let it unfold to reveal a small apron. Every inch was covered in brightly colored embroidery. "For say t'anks," she said, sliding back into old habits. "So happy for knowing much English words."

Emily stared at it, then at Magda, who thrust her hands forward. "Take, take. You like?"

"It's … it's beautiful, but …"

"Mama do …" She seemed to be struggling for a word. "Before," she finally said, "before come here. For Magda's … Magda's …" She shook her head. "Not know how to say. But now it for Emily. For say t'anks."

How can I take this? Emily thought, as a picture of Magda's four gaunt-faced sisters popped into her head. They could sell it for food. But the look on Magda's face stopped her.

"Thank you," she said. "I will treasure it." Magda's face lit up, and she could feel her own face soften. It wasn't Magda's fault, after all, that Dad … She felt tears well up and tried to blink them away. But Magda had noticed and her face puckered anxiously.

"Is wrong to give this?"

"No, no, it's just that I …" I can't. I can't tell her about Dad. If I say it out loud … No. "I'm just tired. That's all." She gave a weak smile, and the anxious frown left Magda's face.

"I know." She nodded. "We all tired. All time tired."

Magda is a good friend, Emily thought, and the tears threatened again. She sped up. "Hurry. We don't want to be late."

But at the sight of the factory, desolation swept over her again. Was this it, for the rest of her life? As Magda climbed the steps to the factory, Emily caught a glimpse of her shoes. Deep cracks ran across each toe and across the soles, too. She looked down at her own neat, black lace-ups. How long before they looked the same? Oh Dad, we counted on you. You promised everything would be all right. You promised.

With a sick feeling, as though her heart was being squeezed by a giant fist, Emily sat down to thread her machine. The women on either side already had their machines humming. Concentrate, Emily told herself. You're already behind. Just get through the day's stint.

Halfway through the morning, a whiff of something acrid made her look up from her work. Was that smoke? Joe and his disgusting cigar, on the prowl again, looking for someone to fine? Earlier that morning he'd shouted at the delivery men when they'd protested his order to stack rolls of fabric up against the fire-escape door, the only free spot in the crowded room. "You'll do as I tell you," Joe had bellowed, his cigar spewing ash as he shook a fist at them, "or you won't be delivering here again."

Emily glanced around. No sign of Joe, but the smell of smoke was stronger now. Where was it coming from?

The woman beside her was sniffing and looking around, too. Suddenly she screamed and pointed. Wisps of smoke drifted up from one of the rolls of fabric in front of the fire-escape door. A tiny flame flickered along the edge of the stiff outer wrapping, then flared. Someone shouted "Fire!" The racket of the sewing machines stopped dead. Before Emily could get to her feet, the narrow aisles were clogged with overturned chairs and shoving women.

For a second she was paralyzed, confused by the screams and stampeding bodies. Then she saw Magda by the fire-escape door. She was struggling to move the smoldering roll of fabric that blocked the way out. Dolly appeared lugging two of the shop's big leather water buckets. Emily darted forward. Together they hoisted one of the heavy buckets and dumped water on the smoking pile. The fire hissed out but, with a muffled "thwump," another bolt burst into flames. Dolly leaped back, and the second bucket tipped, drenching Emily's skirt.

"Get out! Get out!" Dolly shrieked. She grabbed two of the clipping girls and shoved them toward the partially cleared doorway.

Magda appeared beside Emily, towing a coughing Katya. "Take! Take!" She shoved Katya at Emily, then turned back. The three littlest girls were huddled in a far corner.

"Magda! No!" Emily grabbed at her skirt, but Magda slapped her hand away. "Take Katya." And she ran toward the little girls.

Smoke was filling the room. Coughing and choking, Emily grabbed up a corner of her wet skirt and clapped it over Katya's face. She put an arm around the girl's frail shoulders and pushed her toward the doorway. Flames darted at them and Katya flinched. Panic tightened Emily's throat. We can't get through. She half turned. The room was dark with smoke. No sign of Dolly.

We must get out. She tightened her arm around the struggling Katya and lunged past the fiercely burning bolts of cloth. As they burst through the doorway, heat scorched her face. Burning pain ran down her arm. But they were out. She gulped clean air. Katya surged ahead. Hurry, hurry, beat through Emily's brain as they both stumbled down the swaying stairs.

Footsteps pounded behind her, and a thump between the shoulder blades sent her flying. She landed on hands and knees, the cinders of the alleyway digging into her palms. Katya was sprawled beside her. "Get up. Get up." Emily was on her feet pulling at the coughing girl, shoving her along the alleyway toward the street, where a crowd was gathering.

Magda? She turned back. The three little girls came clattering down the stairs. "Where's Magda?" But, wild-eyed, they rushed past her. She looked up. Flames and smoke poured out of the doorway.

The frantic clanging of a bell grew louder, then stopped. "Clear the way! Clear the way!" Men were running up the alley, pulling a long leather hose. Water splattered against the metal stairs and turned to hissing steam.

Emily screamed at them, "Help her! Help her! She's still in there!"

A fireman pushed past her, and she gasped as fiery pain shot down her arm. She put one hand to it and brought away the blackened, charred remains of her sleeve. A deep voice shouted, "There she is."

Emily looked up. Through the thick smoke, a figure appeared on the fire-escape landing. Lit up by flames shooting out broken windows, it stumbled down the first few stairs, face shielded by one arm.

"Magda!"

"Get back!" the deep voice bellowed. Hands dragged Emily away. "It's coming down!"

Emily staggered back as the staircase shuddered and slowly pulled away from the wall. It hung in mid-air for a few seconds. Then it seemed to crumble, raining bits of hot metal onto the silently gaping crowd. From its midst, a bundle of dark clothing tumbled wildly.

"Magda!" Emily ran toward the crumpled figure. "Do something! Do something!" she shrieked, as men with canvas stretchers arrived.

Someone grabbed her by the arm. She screamed as a searing pain shot through her, then everything went black.

The pain woke her. Wildfire scorching her arm, her palms. She lifted one hand, blinking into the darkness. Something white. Large and floppy. A mitten? No — a bandage. Why … ?

Slowly her eyes focused. A hazy blur became the faint outline of a window, the dark oval shape beyond her feet, a footboard. Mam's bed. A gleam of light in the far corner showed a door, slightly ajar. Voices? Who was that?

She rolled onto her side to get a closer look. Pain shot up her arm and she cried out. The door flew open letting in light that dazzled her eyes. She blinked them closed, then she heard Mam's voice.

"At last. You're awake." Emily felt a damp cloth cooling her forehead. "We're so thankful to have you home, Emmy. If it weren't for Miss Henderson … She brought you here from the charity ward, and she's arranged for a visiting nurse."

It was more than Emily could take in. "What …?" she croaked.

"Your poor throat. All that smoke. Don't talk until you've had a drink."

Mam's hand cradled her head and the edge of a glass touched her lips. Water soothed her tongue, her throat, her chest. Then she remembered.

"Magda?"

"I'm so sorry, Emmy."

What did Mam mean? Then she understood. "Dead?"

She didn't need an answer. She had only to close her eyes to see again that figure lying crumpled on the cinders of the alley.

In the days that followed, Emily drifted in and out of sleep, in and out of nightmarish dreams — Joe chasing her with a flaming torch, a great, black bird swooping down at her, only to turn into Magda. She would wake herself screaming, and Mam would come running.

One day she woke to the mouthwatering smell of Mam's soup. But it wasn't Mam this time, it was Ernie standing by her bedside holding the steaming bowl.

"Don't worry about work, Em," he started as soon as her eyes flickered open. "Alf and me are doin' great with the papers. And tomorrow we're off to that fair on the waterfront. We'll do even better there. Hundreds of people. Thousands, maybe. And lots'll want papers."

Work. Soon the bandages would come off, and she would have to do her share. But the thought of work … even lifting her head off the pillow was such an effort. She sank back and closed her eyes.

Another day it was Miss Henderson sitting beside her bed with a stack of books on her lap. "You must read, Emily. It will keep your mind alert."

Her sharp voice was like a hammer tapping on Emily's brain. She knew Miss Henderson meant well, but all she could think was, Please stop.

"I know life is hard for you at the moment," Miss Henderson started gently, then continued in her usual brisk tones, "but you must not give up."

Emily closed her eyes and turned her face away. What was the use? Didn't Miss Henderson understand?

She heard a sigh and the rustle of skirts as Miss Henderson rose.

"I do not intend to let you sink, Emily. You have too much to offer." Then, with a click, the door closed behind her.

Finally one day Mam spoke her mind. "You can't go on

like this, Emily. Your bandages are off, and it's time you got up and faced things."

So here she was, sitting at the table, listlessly sewing buttons onto a coat Ernie had brought from the sweatshop. Helping Mam was all she could manage these days. No hope of work at the factory — the fire had destroyed it. One of these days, of course, she'd have to find work in some other factory. Mam had been so kind. Not pushing. Not criticizing. But soon they would need the money.

She put down her sewing and rubbed her eyes. The room was gloomy despite the bright sun outside, but she couldn't light the lamp this early. Just a waste of oil. She stretched and her glance caught the one bright spot in the room — the intense reds and yellows of the embroidery covering the apron Magda had given her. Mam had spread it out on the dresser, exclaiming over the intricacy of the tiny stitches.

What a miracle it had survived the fire! Folded into a small square, tucked deep into her work apron pocket, it had come through all that turmoil unmarked. If only she could have kept Magda as safe.

Was it my fault? The question haunted Emily. If I'd talked to that lady visitor with the inspector, would it have changed things? If I'd talked to Pete, told him about the scraps lying about and the crowding and the narrow stairs, would that have saved Magda?

A knock at the door interrupted Emily's painful thoughts. Now what? Could she possibly drag herself up to answer it? No one else was at home. Right after breakfast Mam had taken Annie and Bertie to the well-baby clinic at the Settlement House.

More knocking. Louder this time. All right. I'm coming! Irritation gave her the strength to cross the room and open the door.

On the steps stood Pete, cap clutched to his chest.

"Emily, I've got to talk to you. May I come in?"

No, Emily wanted to say, I'm too tired. A minute ago she had regretted not talking to him. Now he was the last person she wanted to see. Not knowing what else to do, she stepped back. He took that as an invitation, but once inside he waited until she gestured toward a chair. Then he sat silently, staring at the floor, twisting his cap in his hands.

Unwilling to break the silence, she had reached for her sewing when he burst out, "I went to see Magda's family. Oh, Emily — it was dreadful."

Startled, she looked up, but he was still staring at the floor.

"It was hard to find them. Finally Katya took me. Down a back alley. The father barely speaks English. And there were hordes of children. Some other families were there, crowded into that horrible cellar."

Emily shivered, remembering the wan little sisters. The unlit stove. The stomach-turning smells.

"I've never seen people live like that," Pete began again. "My editor just laughed when I told him. 'Toughen up, kid,' he said. 'Reporters see worse than that every day.' But if reporters see it, Emily, they should do something about it, shouldn't they?"

She felt tongue-tied, but Pete didn't wait for an answer.

"I've been thinking about it a lot, especially since I …" He pulled a crumpled handbill from his pocket, smoothed it and held it out to Emily. "I went to the rally — you know, to hear Clara Lemlich. She was electrifying, Emily. She talked about working together to make things better. They did that in New York, she says. They demanded shorter hours. Higher wages. And better treatment from bosses."

"They got all that?"

"No, not all of it. But they made a start. They were listened to."

Emily turned back to the picture of the fiery-eyed Clara. You could tell she was a fighter. No hesitancy in her face. No wondering what or if. Just bulldog determination.

Like Magda, Emily thought, remembering how Magda had struggled to keep her little sisters fed, to learn English and, that last day, to clear every one of the clipping girls out of the burning room. Yes, Magda was another fighter. But it had all been for nothing.

With a deep sigh Emily dropped the handbill onto the table, but Clara's eyes seemed to follow her. Why should it all be for nothing, they demanded? You can do something.

"But what?" she blurted out. "What can I do?"

Pete looked up, frowning. "What are you talking about?"

But Emily was lost in her thoughts. "After all, I'm only one person." She was on her feet now, pacing around the table. "The other girls can't help. They're too scared, too exhausted. Besides, they can't speak English."

She stopped in front of Pete, her hands on her hips. "There is nothing I can do," she said, as though he were demanding something of her. "Except …"

She paused, an idea just beginning to form. She sat down across from Pete and slowly worked it out in her mind.

The other girls know about the little girls in the box and how dangerous the stairs were and how Magda had to care for three little sisters all by herself. But I'm the only one who can actually tell the story.

"Maybe you're right. I do need to talk to you … to your newspaper." She reached for the apron and spread it lovingly on the table. "If people knew about the factories and the way working girls have to live, maybe they *would* change things."

"Wait. Just let me get my notebook." As Pete fumbled in his pocket, Emily was arranging the words in her head. Even before he had his pencil poised she knew what she wanted to say.

"Let me tell you about my friend Magda …" she began.

A FIRE THAT MADE A DIFFERENCE

"Fire! Fire! Read all about it! Factory fire kills twelve!"

In cities all over North America newsboys shouted similar headlines. For them it meant selling more papers. But for the factory workers fires meant, at best, no work while the damaged factory was repaired and, at worst, severe injuries or even death. Fires in the crowded factory districts were so common that most people paid no attention, but in 1911 in New York City one factory fire had important consequences.

Horse-drawn fire engines raced to the fire at the Triangle Shirtwaist Factory.

Late one March afternoon clanging fire trucks sped through the factory district of New York to a ten-story building that housed the Triangle Shirtwaist Factory. As the firemen unreeled their hoses, screams made them look up. Frantically waving young women leaned from ninth-floor windows. Around them swirled flames and black smoke. The firemen hoisted their ladders, but not one was long enough to reach the ninth floor. To the horror of onlookers unable to help, the screaming girls climbed out on the ledges. Within seconds, bodies were hurtling through the air and thudding onto the pavement. In all, 146 people, most of them teenaged girls from immigrant families, died that day.

The details of those gruesome deaths, reported in all the newspapers, sickened New Yorkers. They demanded to know how this could happen. The result was a famous trial in which the factory owners were charged with negligence (lack of proper care and attention).

What had happened in the few minutes before fire engulfed the entire floor? Some workers had escaped. Why hadn't others? As survivor after survivor was called to testify, a grim picture of working conditions in the factory was revealed.

At the Triangle factory, the girls reported, it was common practice for scraps of fabric and discarded bits of paper patterns to be thrown into boxes under the tables and kept there for weeks. A spark from careless smoking could turn these boxes into fire bombs — and the men in the cutting room were allowed to smoke on the job.

Hosing down the building proved useless.

It was also common practice to lock the doors so the forelady could monitor trips to the washroom. At the end of each day workers were ordered to line up at the locked door to be searched for any scraps of lace or fabric they might have stolen. Did a locked door, that fatal March day, cause a bottleneck of workers, making it impossible for more than a few to escape down the stairs?

Charred tables and chairs are all that remain of the room where the young seamstresses worked.

After many months of hearing the evidence, the judge and jury concluded that the lawyers had not proved conclusively that the doors had been locked that afternoon. The owners, the judge ruled, were not to blame.

The public was shocked and outraged. If the owners were not guilty, then who was?

Factory fires were common in North America. Workers often died. But it took the dramatic images of girls plunging to their deaths from ninth-story windows to make the public pay attention. At long last the lawmakers were listening to the reformers. Even so, this was just the beginning of a long fight to make factories safe.

FIGHTING FOR A FAIR DEAL

Emily was shocked when Magda shrugged her shoulders and declared "Boss make rules." But Magda had worked longer than Emily. She knew some of the cruel truths about factory work in 1912. She knew that if she quit, or if Joe fired her, there would always be someone waiting to take her place. She also knew that, even if she found another factory job, the conditions would be the same. And Magda and the other girls had a stronger reason for putting up with Joe and the unfairness of life. In their factory they had friends, people to talk to, to share both their troubles and their hopes for the future. They were no longer strangers in a strange land.

Marching in a labor parade, these girls display banners in English and Yiddish calling on governments to abolish child slavery in factories.

Not everyone was as resigned as Magda. Some girls in factories and mills found the conditions intolerable. Gradually they came up with ideas about how they could make changes happen. Two words would make this all possible — "strike" and "union."

STRIKES

Workers realized that the factory owners needed them just as much as the workers needed jobs. Replacing five or six workers might be easy, but what if suddenly the owners had no workers at all?

This idea led to strikes. At a prearranged time every worker would turn off her machine and walk out of the factory. No one would return until the owner agreed to listen to their grievances.

Strikes worked. Owners usually had to give in. But when strikes dragged on for days or weeks, the hardships for workers were severe. Surely there was a less disruptive way of getting the owners' attention. One answer was to form unions.

UNIONS

"Union" means "join together." Workers joined together to negotiate pay increases and improvements to their working conditions. They elected two or three leaders to conduct the bargaining. If the boss refused their demands, the leaders might advise the workers to strike. A surprising number of union leaders in the garment industry were teenaged girls, like Clara Lemlich.

CLARA LEMLICH

"I vote we go on a general strike."

The crowd of 3000 female garment workers erupted in cheers. They stamped their feet, whistled, waved handkerchiefs and shouted to show their approval for the woman on the stage. Tiny but determined, Clara Lemlich was only twenty-three that day in 1909 when she climbed on the stage of the Cooper Union building in New York City. But she was already an old hand at stirring up audiences. She had been organizing strikes since she was seventeen.

Clara's life story was similar to that of many of the immigrant girls and women who became active reformers. She was born in a *shtetl* (the Jewish section of a town or village) in the Ukrainian town of Gorodok. While her father and brothers spent each day studying the Torah, Clara, with her mother and sisters, ran a small shop to support the family. Hungry for the education denied girls in her culture, she earned money writing letters for illiterate neighbors so she could buy books.

In 1903 Clara and her family joined the millions of European Jews immigrating to

America. In the crowded industrial district of New York, Clara and her sisters found jobs in garment factories.

Clara was a gifted seamstress. Even as a teenager she earned a good wage as a draper (see page 38). Despite her privileged position, she was disgusted by the conditions in factories. It was bad enough that bosses paid so poorly, but the worst indignity came at the end of each day when workers had to line up to be searched to make sure no one had stolen a piece of lace or a scrap of material.

Clara Lemlich

Clara was determined to stop this exploitation. She was convinced one person alone could do nothing. Workers had power only if they stood together and, with one voice, demanded change. Moving from factory to factory, she preached this message. On the day of the Cooper Union meeting she had come to the end of her patience. Strikes by small groups of workers weren't working. The time had come for every garment worker in every factory in the city to walk out. Only a coordinated effort would give them a strong enough voice.

Bosses realized the danger. They hired thugs to beat up the strikers. Clara became a target. One night she was followed and beaten by two burly men. They left her bleeding on the sidewalk. But the pain of six broken ribs did not deter Clara. She used her bruises to stir her comrades to greater fury. Within days of the savage beating she was back on street corners preaching, "Strike! Strike! Strike!" And when she called for a general strike, the other garment workers listened. "Ah, then," Clara said late in her life, "then I had fire in my mouth."

Clara and the many other immigrant girls who bravely refused to be exploited by the factory owners were the driving force behind factory reform. Despite the efforts of well-to-do women to reform the factory system, it was the workers themselves who forced the government to pass laws that made factories safer and fairer.

LOOKING TO THE FUTURE

Children have always worked. But as work moved from homes and small craft shops into factories with dangerous machinery, their working lives became both tedious and dangerous.

Change came slowly in the factories. It took years of lobbying on the part of many people, including the children themselves, to improve the working and living conditions of the poor. Gradually cities forced landlords to clean up the slums, and governments at all levels passed laws that kept children out of factories so that they could go to school. This didn't happen fast enough for Emily and her friends and siblings. They were the fighters who worked with reporters like Pete and through labor unions to make things better for the workers who came after them.

In North America the battle has almost been won. But even today there is still some child labor. In rural areas children of migrant workers are kept out of school to help with harvesting. And in cities, after school and on weekends, some children still work long hours in sweatshops. But most children in North America are now able to enjoy their childhood years and, just as important, stay in school long enough to get the education and training they need to become successful adult workers.

But what about other parts of the world? In countries such as India, Pakistan, China and other Asian countries many thousands of children, some as young as six, work long hours in sweatshop conditions. They work at many types of jobs, but the most notorious is carpet weaving. Tiny fingers are nimble at tying the thousands of knots that make up one carpet. But those fingers can also become swollen, scarred and gnarled by the endless work, and hunching over to work in confined spaces permanently twists the spines of young workers. Why do they do it? For the same reason that Emily and Magda had to work — without their wages their families would starve.

There is a solution: education. Many conditions need to change in these countries, but experience has shown that when governments provide free schooling, books, uniforms and, most importantly, meals, many more families can afford to let their children attend school.

North American children, for the most part, are now able to enjoy their childhood as they grow into educated adults. One battle has been won, but in other parts of the world the fight continues.

In Kabul, Afghanistan, a
thirteen-year-old boy sews
a pair of pants while a seven-
year-old checks the stitching.
The boys work in the tailor
shop every day after school.

THE LONG FIGHT

1853 – The first effective laws on child labor are passed in Prussia (Germany). By 1900 many European countries have similar laws.

1919 – The International Labor Organization is founded. It works toward ending child labor.

1938 – The Fair Labor Standards Act is passed, the first successful federal legislation on child labor in the United States.

1946 – The United Nations International Children's Emergency Fund (UNICEF) is founded.

1989 – The United Nations Convention on the Rights of the Child, created to protect such basic rights as the right to education, shelter and safety, was ratified (passed into law) by all but two of the 189 nations in the U.N. The United States is one nation that has not yet ratified the Convention.

1990 – Operation Child Watch is initiated by the United States Labor Department in an attempt to restrict child labor.

1995 – Child activist and former carpet weaver Iqbal Masih, aged fourteen, is murdered in Pakistan.

1995 – Craig Kielburger, aged twelve, founds Free the Children to focus attention on the plight of child workers in carpet factories. By 2003 the organization has 10 000 members in thirty-five countries and now concentrates on education and development projects.

1996 – The First International Meeting of Working Children is held in Kundapur, India.

2004 – The first Children's World Congress is held in Florence, Italy, where 150 child delegates from fifty countries speak about the social problems that arise from child labor. The participants are encouraged to become activists for children's rights.

2005 – The second Children's World Congress is held in New Delhi, India, to encourage participation from children in Asia and Africa who could not attend the first congress.

GLOSSARY

assembly line — a row of workers or machines along which work is passed until the final product is completed

conveyor belt — a mechanical device that carries things from one place to another; an endless, moving belt

garment — any article of clothing

handbill — a printed announcement or advertisement to be handed out to people

immigrant — a person who moves to a country to live permanently

seamstress — a woman whose work is sewing

shirtwaist — a woman's blouse with details copied from men's shirts

slum — a crowded, run-down part of a city marked by poverty

stint — the amount of work a factory worker was expected to do each hour or each day

strike — a stopping of work by employees who hope to pressure the employer into giving them more pay, shorter hours or better working conditions

sweatshop — a factory in which workers are employed for long hours at low pay in unhealthy conditions

tailor's dummy — a form shaped like a human figure, used by tailors to model clothes on

tenement — an apartment building, usually in poor condition and overcrowded

union — a group of workers joined together to protect and promote their interests

INDEX